AWAKEN THE CREATOR WITHIN
ASCEND TO YOUR HIGHEST REALITY

ROBIN DAVIS

DIVINE DESTINY PUBLISHING

Copyright © 2022 by Robin Davis and Divine Destiny Publishing

All Rights Reserved. Apart from any fair dealing for the purposes of research or private study, or criticism or review, as permitted under the Copyright, Designs and Patents Act 1988, this publication may only be reproduced, stored or transmitted, in any form or by any means, with the prior permission in writing of the copyright owner, or in the case of the reprographic reproduction in accordance with the terms of licensees issued by the Copyright Licensing Agency. Enquiries concerning reproduction outside those terms should be sent to the publisher.

CONTENTS

Introduction v

1. **Chapter 1** 1
   Introduction to Beliefs
2. **Chapter 2** 5
   Beliefs – Plato's Allegory of the Cave
3. **Chapter 3** 14
   Our Thoughts Create Our Reality
4. **Chapter 4** 24
   Emotional Scale of Consciousness and Our Vibrational Energy
5. **Chapter 5** 38
   Hierarchy of Needs
6. **Chapter 6** 61
   Values and Intention
7. **Chapter 7** 70
   Self Concept and Identity
8. **Chapter 8** 78
   Self Confidence and Trust
9. **Chapter 9** 83
   Bridge of Incidents
10. **Chapter 10** 107
    Imagination
11. **Chapter 11** 122
    Focus and Priming
12. **Chapter 12** 131
    Auto Suggestion and Hypnosis
13. **Chapter 13** 141
    Summary of Activities

14. Conclusion 148
15. About The Author 151
    Robin Davis

    Resources and References 153

INTRODUCTION

It's September 8, of 2022 and I'm on a flight to Barcelona. I'm traveling to the Spanish Pyrenees for a week-long expedition with Wim Hof aka The Iceman.

My intentions are very clear.

1. Let go of everything, people, places, things, beliefs and habits that have been holding me back from living my life fearlessly.

2. Find out why I can't lose weight.

3. Most importantly, have a better relationship with myself.

You see, I've come to understand something profoundly strange about the world. It is a reflection of who I believe I am, and who I believe others are.

A mirror of my own subconscious thoughts, beliefs, and feelings. The past five years I've been on a quest to look deeply into the mirror without fear, shame, guilt, regret, pain, sorrow and understand the reflection, so I can adjust it.

Imagine looking into a mirror and seeing something off about your appearance. You wouldn't touch the mirror to fix it. You would adjust it on your person and then the mirror would reflect the change back to you.

Changing yourself sounds easy, but for those of us who grew up experiencing trauma, poverty and lack we are all weighed down with societal belief structures that subconsciously affect our ability to think and see things clearly never-mind change ourselves.

Let's take one belief structure or template as I call it. In the Catholic Church, the set of beliefs that have been stacked like a pair of sunglasses on our face, significantly distorts our view of the world/reality.

Politics is another set of belief structures or templates that are forced on us. Depending on the community you grew up in, and the set of values those in a position of power have, determines the morals/values we will tend to mimic in order for external validation and acceptance in society. We are taught early on in childhood to follow societal norms in order to fit in and be accepted by the masses and obtain approval from the leaders in the hierarchical tribe. The pattern of this behavior is built in our DNA for survival. So trying to blame or shame these institutions is pointless. One must accept our role in going along with it for survival and go about reprogramming or deprogramming these belief structures in ourselves.

INTRODUCTION

Growing up in Northeastern Pennsylvania, I socially identified as an Irish, Catholic, Democrat. Poor or at least in the lower middle class. If you didn't go without electricity for a few months, or heat or hot water or fight over who is going to eat the last of whatever was for dinner or sneak food into your room after meals because you were still hungry, then count yourself among the higher echelon of society. Growing up this way only weighed me down even more with shame. It wasn't until a year or so ago that I could even talk about the way that I grew up publicly.

I was born into a number of limiting belief structures. And I had no idea how negatively it would impact my entire life until a few short years ago, when I was diagnosed with cancer.

I mentioned that I was Irish. Let me explain what I found about my culture. A few years ago I realized I was just another woman in my ancestral lineage who was born into a cycle of addiction, codependency and abuse. You see, as far back as I can confirm, there has been a history of the women in my lineage who marry abusive, toxic addicts, who then have children and keep that cycle of toxicity going. Even I succumbed to this and brought three beautiful babies into the world under the same set of circumstances as my mother, my mother's mother, and I suspect it goes further back to my ancestors in Ireland.

Now there's something to be said as well about depression being passed on genetically. Irish immigrants spent long hard days in the coal mines of Pa where I grew up.

Lack of Vitamin D stemming from daylight deprivation certainly didn't help the depressive circumstances here in America, the so-called land of opportunity.

Now let me stop here and assure you, the reader, something very important. I take full responsibility for all my decisions and actions regardless of how I grew up. As an adult, I had my own mind. And this book isn't about blaming society. This book is about understanding it and understanding ourselves and making better choices.

It's about waking up.

So I'm on this plane, and I'm ready to land in Barcelona. Meeting 100+ other participants and Wim's team to take us to our camp in the Pyrenees Mountains. It's the first time I have a sense of dread and something feels off with me.

In the weeks prior, I did have a sense of nervousness about the ice baths. I extremely dislike the cold so I was a little nervous I wouldn't be able to complete those. But as far as anything else coming up, I'm a former Marine, a badass. I've kicked cancer's ass. I'm super confident that I can handle anything but the nervousness lingered with me through the flight and while I was meeting my group mates. We arrived at Camp, unpacked and I quickly slid into bed. I slept great, I think because I was so exhausted.

We started the next day with breakfast and then we were on our way to the first group ice bath with the Iceman himself. We had some down time before the ice baths, so our team leads began a guided breathwork session. It started out as a beautiful, relaxing meditation on the green lush grass under the beautiful sun and turned out to be the start of a long emotional roller coaster.

During the meditation I had a realization that I hadn't been in my body completely since I was a child. Guilt, shame and fear hit me like a ton of bricks.

And I realized my entire life I had been running from my feelings, running towards anything that would numb out the feelings I tried so hard to ignore. I used alcohol, drugs, psychedelics, sex and a big one was food to numb my body so I didn't have to feel.

I cried during this meditation as this realization came into my awareness. I shared briefly with the group what I was feeling and then we were off to the ice baths. Much to my surprise, I knocked the ice beds out of the park. Who knew that all the years of disassociating with my reality just to survive, so that I could pretend my circumstances weren't real, would make the Wim Hof ice baths a walk in the park.

Things began unraveling after that.

I did ask to have a better relationship with myself. I didn't realize I'd be leaving not only with that, but with the number one tool to process and resolve my trauma.

Over the course of the next week, I basically cried every day. I forced myself to stay in my body, follow through with the breathing and the work we were doing and faced my emotions head on. Thankfully, on the last day I woke up refreshed. I wasn't crying.

One of those nights when I was so exhausted, I thought for sure I would fall asleep quickly. But I tossed and turned. My body ached, not just from the activities that we had been doing like hiking and canyoning, but I had this all over body pain that I couldn't ignore.

Two scenarios kept coming to mind. The first one was when I was 17 years old.

I had a caregiver who physically and verbally abused me since I was seven years old. Now, a few days prior to this scenario, they had punched me in the face and busted my nose. So here I was again and they were taunting me trying to elicit an emotional reaction. You see they just wanted the POWER to hurt me. Any evidence of emotion on my part got them off. So I learned how to stuff down my emotions and pretend nothing was happening. Pretend those words or fists didn't hurt me. The problem though, is it only enraged this person and their behavior escalated. I tried so hard to ignore the taunts and the slaps in the side of my head, but their behavior kept escalating, saying worse things and the hits were getting harder. I knew it was only a matter of seconds before he hit me in the face.

I was standing over the sink washing dishes. My hands were in the sink, they were on the other side of the sink.

I snapped.

I don't know what came over me but I pulled a steak knife out of the water and motioned towards him.

He laughed. He actually laughed at me and told me I was a weak little girl. "What are you going to do?"

I responded that I wouldn't do anything right then and there. I would wait until he fell asleep.

It was then that he realized how serious I was. He stammered backwards and I said "Go ahead, hit me. I dare you".

He walked away muttering to himself. That was the last day he ever said anything negative to me or touched me again.

I later joined the Marines and you would think I would have learned my lesson. But no. Fast forward to 2006, I'm married with three kids. I found out that my husband was cheating on me for several years and gaslighting me about it. I knew and yet I ignored the red flags.

He was a recovering alcoholic. 'Recovering', just meant he didn't drink anymore. He had never dealt with the addictive behaviors or the reasons he drank. Those were left untreated and he just became worse and worse over time. He didn't drink alcohol, but his addictive behavior just rotated from sex to porn, to drugs, to work to working out, etc.

The anger he had inside began creeping out more and more over time. He became explosive and reactive, leaving our lives miserable.

In the second scenario that I kept going over in my head at Wim Hof, I kept returning to the first time I tried to leave him. He was smashing things around the house. Trying to get me to react... sound familiar? Trying to make me cry. I'd had enough. I yelled up to the kids to pack a bag and that I was going to take them to his mother's for the night. We weren't going to stay there if he was acting like this.

I walked into my bedroom/bathroom to get some things.

I heard the basement door open, it was right next to my bedroom. I heard him go down a few steps and stop.

Above the steps was a shelf where he kept all of his guns.

I stood still and just listened. I heard the shotgun open. I heard him load the shells and snap it shut.

Everything happened so fast after that.

He began ranting and raving that I wasn't leaving. That he'd kill me and burn the house down around my body.

The next thing I know I was on the floor in the corner of the bathroom. The left side of my face was pressed up against the cold tile, the end of the shotgun barrel digging into the right side of my temple. My eyes are closed. He had closed the door and locked it on his way in. My kids were on the other side screaming and crying. My oldest jumped up and grabbed the key that we kept on the top of the door trim and opened it. She tried to talk to him, but he wouldn't stop. That's when she ran and grabbed the phone to call his mom. She only lived a few miles away. She came in and talked him down. Took the gun and us to her house.

At first she was enraged and determined that we all needed to get away from him when he was being a monster. But then after a few days she pulled me aside and told me to go home. That he loved me. And she said "Just don't do anything to make him mad again."

By the way, this is the same thing my mother told me when I told her about my childhood abuse, "Don't do anything to make him mad".

I eventually did leave.

I got a PFA (Protection From Abuse order). And he did end up going to jail for stalking, harassing and abusing me. But here's the thing. While my mind forgave my abusers a long time ago, my body did not.

INTRODUCTION

During the night at Wim Hof, the pain in my body kept getting worse. I hardly slept at all. I woke up sobbing.

All the work I'd done over the past five, six years and we're back to square one?! Still going over the trauma in the past?

I was so angry. It's like all the work was for nothing. I felt like crap but I forced myself to go to breathwork with Wim because I made a promise to myself.

It was raining that day, which made it even worse. I could barely hold it together, could barely hold my tears back in front of everyone.

I laid out my mat and my sleeping bag and tucked myself in. I was here and maybe I'll just sleep. But as we began meditating I began to relax. And then Wim begins our breathwork session.

"Fully in, and fully out. Let the body do what the body does. Let go of all the trauma...."

As I followed the breath in and out, all I could feel was the most intense pain. Electrifying pain leaving my body. I cried so hard. I pulled my sleeping bag over my face. I couldn't even keep pace with Wim, the pain was so excruciating. I could literally feel it coming from my core, radiating out of my body, as if knives were being pulled out.

This breathwork nearly did me in.

When the breathwork session was over, I curled up on my side and just cried. I had hidden the pain and the shame away in my body all these years. I had never processed it. I can see now I was afraid to acknowledge it. Afraid if I acknowledged it, I would somehow find out that everything they ever said to me about me was true. What if there really was something wrong with me? What if I deserve to be treated that way? What if all my fears were true? I kept those shameful secrets locked away for years.

I'm finally in a place where they cannot hurt me anymore. It was time to realize them and release them.

Why tell you all this and then have you read on?

You picked up this book in hopes of healing your own life or your own trauma.

You have one of the keys now. It's breathwork.

So why read on?

Because I had intense trauma that my subconscious has been protecting me from facing all these years. It wasn't until I was mentally strong enough to handle it, that it came out through breathwork.

How did I become mentally strong? Well read on.

Knowing the tools and the techniques in this book will help everyone on the planet.

If you're in an abusive situation, there are resources that can help you please consider contacting the National Domestic Violence Hotline in the US at: 800-799-7233 for help.

I promise you there is a way out.

I found it.

And I saved myself and my kids.

CHAPTER 1

INTRODUCTION TO BELIEFS

I am going to become the person that I want to be. I am going to throw off all of the shackles, all of the beliefs, all of those outdated templates that no longer serve me. I am going to disregard the way that society has told me including what I should be doing and I am going to be who I want to be.

I am going to show up in the world how I want to show up. I am going to do the things that I want to do with a no f's given attitude. And by following the steps outlined in this book, you can transform your life too.

After emerging from a crisis of identity, I made the biggest commitment that I have ever made in my life. It is changing my life for the better and it will change yours too.

I am committed to doing whatever it will take. It did not matter how long it took, it did not matter how much it would cost. None of those things mattered. I committed. I am in this for the long haul and am sharing this journey to benefit others.

I have spent the past few years tearing down the belief templates that had been programmed in me by the world around me.

It was such a revelation to discover I only needed to embrace who I already was. The real me. The me before society told me to be someone else, told me to conform, to be like everyone else.

I spent the past few years learning how to BE me.

There are many different 'belief templates.' Think of religion, politics, family structure, grade school, high school, college, work, etc. Every system has belief templates in place. We grow up and learn to fit into those templates, so we can 'fit' into our world, our society.

All beliefs and belief templates are limiting, except for one.

I am.

"I am," is the only belief in our reality that takes into account the infinite, diverse human being that I am. It implies that I am EVERYTHING.

All other beliefs are somewhat limiting.

If I say, I am abundant, this limits who I am.

If I say, I am loved, this limits who I am.

It implies that other parts of me are limited or do not exist.

The best affirmation you can use is "I am."

But until you identify the limiting beliefs you have about yourself; you may be fighting an uphill battle trying to reprogram your mind.

In this book, I will walk you through reality, how to identify and smash your limiting beliefs and reprogram your mind to embrace the infinite being you are.

You can say this is the ULTIMATE guide to Mastering your Mind, to Master your Reality.

What you will need:

1. Journal

2. Pen/Pencil

3. Open Mind

4. Willingness to change

You do not need to believe everything in this book in order to be successful but having an open mind and a willingness to change is key. I wrote this book to help people shift their consciousness, to expand and grow, to consider new possibilities.

When working with belief systems and templates, I have found that people, including myself, initially resist changing their mindset. But once they start accepting it, it becomes easier and easier to do. With some belief systems, our brains will convince us that we will die if we give up a specific belief. That is how our brain is designed to protect us. As you go through this process and your brain gathers evidence that you will not die, you will embrace new thoughts, new ideas and more expansive beliefs like you have never done before.

No matter how hard it gets for you, make a commitment that you will complete the book and the activities.

I promise, you will not be disappointed.

There are loads of resources for you that I will share.

Including hypnosis sessions, meditations, affirmations to pair with the book. All designed to give you optimal results.

You can find the resources here: https://www.lifemasterywithrobin.com/book

As always, I love you. You got this! Keep going!

CHAPTER 2

BELIEFS – PLATO'S ALLEGORY OF THE CAVE

"It is the task of the Enlightened not only to ascend learning and to see the good, but to be willing to descend again to those prisoners and to share their troubles and their honors. Whether they are worth having or not. In this they must do even with the prospect of death."— **Plato**

"All that we are is a result of what we have thought." —**Buddha**

"If a man looks upon any other man and estimates that man as less than himself, then he is stealing from the other. He is stealing the other's birthright - that of equality."

— **Neville Goddard**

When we are faced with a limiting belief, and challenged to change it, our brains distort the consequences and can make us feel like we will die if we give up that belief.

Plato's cave begins with a description of people in a deep cave, but people are bound and can only look forward. Now behind them is a wall, and then high above that and behind them is a fire. Passing between the fire and the wall are people and objects that are casting shadows on the wall that the prisoners are forced to watch.

The prisoners believe that they are witnessing the world, but they are only seeing the distorted shadows of the beings and the things moving behind them, not the things as they are or the sounds that they hear are just distorted sounds as well bouncing off the cave wall, not the actual sound. (See Plato's Cave illustration)

Here is an illustration of Plato's Cave:

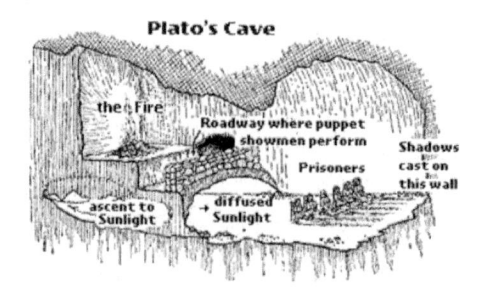

Plato's allegory of the cave: https://faculty.washington.edu/smcohen/320/cave.htm

One of the prisoners gets away and he climbs out of the cave and goes outside, looks around, sees the sunlight, sees how shadows are actually made. Sees an entire new world, hears, feels, touches, smells, all of his senses are filled with brand new sensations. He runs back down into the cave to tell the other prisoners what he saw.

The remaining prisoners were so adamant in their beliefs, unwilling to change those beliefs. This is how they grew up. This is all they knew of society. This is what was passed down to them. This is what they experienced every single day, and this is how they translated the world around them. Instead of admitting that they could possibly be wrong, that there could possibly be more out there than what they were translating within the cave, they killed the prisoner.

The only way that they would have faced the truth is if someone unchained them and dragged them up to see for themselves, but they were unwilling to even consider for a second that that prisoner was correct. Because it went against every belief that they had it threatened their entire survival.

This is a dramatic example of challenging a limiting belief. In the cave those faced with the challenge to change it, distorted the consequences by killing someone rather than give up that belief.

By the time we are seven, most of our beliefs about the world are formed in our minds, shaped by the caregivers and the society that we grew up in. As we get older, those beliefs become reinforced.

We learn these things also from the people that we love. The beliefs become entrenched. We are willing to defend and fight for those beliefs. In Platos' story, the prisoners were willing to kill to protect their beliefs.

I think we do this out of fear - fear that our reality as we know it was wrong. Or the caregivers - our parents, grandparents, friends, community were wrong. This threatens our identity. What does it say about me if these beliefs aren't true? Does it mean I'm stupid? Does it mean my parents are dumb? Does it mean something is wrong with me?!

When my beliefs were threatened in the past, it brought so much shame up in me. Shame about the way I grew up. Shame about my parents and lack of having the best parental guidance.

When that shame came up for me, I dug into my old belief systems even more. I desperately needed to protect them and my identity.

Another reason we cannot let them go is because the risk of facing it, looking at it, trying to debunk it might just prove to us that a limiting belief is true.

I may have a belief that I am stupid, I am unloved, or I am unwanted. If I decide to look at that belief to try to debunk it, my fear will kick up. I am going to run from discovering whether that is true or not. Because if it is true that would mean that I am stupid, I am unloved or I am unwanted.

I consider that I have invested so much in my (limited) belief I feel I would die if I changed it I would end. So, our ego does not want to try to debunk those beliefs out of fear of death, out of fear of facing that there really is something wrong with us.

Have you ever argued or witnessed people arguing on social media about politics? There is NO CHANCE either side will see the error of their ways and admit someone else is right. No one has ever changed their mind by arguing about a subject on social media. In fact, it gets quite nasty. Because when a person's reality is threatened, they feel their life is threatened. Hence they will become more and more defensive and argumentative.

The allegory is an exploration of truth and how those with different experiences or backgrounds may perceive reality. Some may translate it very differently. Each of us is out here in this world translating reality uniquely. The way we were influenced as we grew up in our society, the influence of our parents and our caregivers as well as our religion or culture, has defined our beliefs.

Anyone coming in and challenging that should fear death. The allegory is basically showing us that every one of us is wrong. We only can "SEE" our version of truth based on our state of being/consciousness.

We all are interpreting reality, through our own eyes. Everything that we see is an illusion.

Look at the teachers that we have had in our lives. Our parents, our teachers, our society, our church. Everyone that was teaching us about reality. They were only teaching us from their perspective, from their view, therefore, even what we are learning from society and from others, is incorrect.

Growing up most of my beliefs were told to me and I believed that was just the way it was. It was not until I got older that I started to live and experience the truth of my life, the truth of my being. There was nothing in my belief system that I discovered on my own until I was older while raising and teaching my own family.

Prior to that all my beliefs were adopted from other people who told me the "truth". Well, their truth.

I had someone I loved very much when I was growing up who taught me a lot of really good things, but this person was extremely racist. Not because they had a negative experience with a non-white person. Because that is what was passed down to them. That is what was told to them.

Now thankfully, I have had the benefit of other people in my life who were able to counter those particular beliefs. I also knew in my heart that the limiting beliefs were not true.

Imagine people that grow up with beliefs about hate. Those beliefs will continue to be passed down to them and will continue to perpetuate unless someone in that family/society raises their consciousness and begins teaching love.

The people in the cave, when those shadows appear, they contrive a certain meaning as to what those shadows are. They make up an entire story. They give meaning to something they do not even see clearly or distinctly. They have concocted an entire story about those shadows and about those sounds. And they are willing to kill to protect their beliefs.

Sound familiar? I can recall many examples in history that support this. But this book is not about that.

The level of education that a person receives, is based on how conscious the teacher and the student is. The teacher can be very wise and all-knowing and the student unconscious. Both can be completely unconscious. Or the teacher could be unconscious and the student perhaps a little wiser. Unconscious in lacking awareness, ignorant on certain topics and needing to be enlightened.

I think in my case my internal guidance system alerted me at times when the information I was hearing from teachers, caregivers and society was off, but I ignored it.

Humans live in this world, only interpreting the circumstances that they observe and nothing more. Our unenlightened state of driving that interpretation.

People's observation, with no real insight to what is passed down to them perpetuates limited states of awareness.

When I was 5 years old, I had a teacher in religion class tell me, "Bad things happen to bad people". This distorted my entire view of both the world and myself for a very long time. It distorted my view of reality. I immediately had a fear of becoming a bad person, because I did not want bad things to happen.

Having been brought up in the Catholic Church, we learned you would burn in Hell... so that was a good reason as any to be good.

But for the longest time, most of my life in fact, when bad things happened to me, I believed that it was because I was a bad person.

Why oh why would a high-level member in a church teach that to an impressionable five-year-old and no one would disagree with that? No one objected. It was further reinforced when I watched the news or listened to adults gossiping. So and so was arrested for this, so and so is getting divorced because they are a drinker and so on.

Bad things happened to bad people. So as negative things were happening in my life, I was convinced it must be that I was a bad person. I believed this because there were many (negative) unwanted situations in my life. Therefore, most of my life I walked around thinking I was a bad person.

My beliefs about always being poor were instilled from an early age.

I was taught I would never leave the poor/middle class, that I would never amount to anything in life.

There were caregivers that would tell me how useless I was. You are dumb. You are fat. You are lazy. You are stupid. You will never be anything better. You are never going to go anywhere in life. You are a loser.

The sad part is that I believed them for a long time.

Many people in our society today are like the people in the cave. Their only sense of "reality" is what they observe from a limited perspective. And the stories they are told reinforce their narrow and misguided views.

They are forced unsuspectingly to believe limiting stories. They hold limiting beliefs about themselves and their lives, and what reality is. And they will spew purported facts to support those limiting beliefs. They will cling to them. They will argue for their limitations. Because in some cases, it would mean, when beliefs are challenged, that they are going to die. They subconsciously believe

"If I give up this belief, I will die". And those people in the cave chose to kill the other prisoner rather than face the truth. A case of let's shoot the messenger!

So, when we start to look at these limiting beliefs, we are going to take it one aspect at a time. We are going to ease ourselves into safety and get comfortable by using a mirror to identify our limiting beliefs, changing them, replacing them and letting them go.

ACTIVITY:

1. Identify 10 beliefs you had as a child that you learned were untrue as an adult.

2. Identify your thoughts on the reason(s) you were taught those beliefs. Don't be judgmental on this. Try to identify the root of the reasoning. In most cases it's out of fear. But Fear of what?

3. Give yourself permission to explore more ideas and beliefs that you've learned in your life, that may not be true or real.

CHAPTER 3

OUR THOUGHTS CREATE OUR REALITY

"Assume the feeling of your *wish fulfilled and observe the route that your attention follows.*"

— Neville Goddard, The Power of Awareness

"*Nothing comes from without; all things come from within - from the subconscious*"

— Neville Goddard, Resurrection

"*Everything you want is out there waiting for you to ask. Everything you want also wants you. But you have to take action to get it.*" — Jack Canfield

There is a study that was done not long ago where they had actors walk up to one hundred people at a park. Each time, the actor would reach into their pocket to get their phone and ask the stranger to hold their coffee. The actor gets their phone out, looks at it and then takes their coffee back from the stranger. Fifty of the cases were hot coffee and fifty were cold coffee.

Thirty minutes later, someone approaches the stranger again with a clipboard and gives them $20.00 and asks, "If you will give me a minute of your time to read this three-paragraph story and answer these two questions, this money is yours." The strangers read the story, answer the questions, and take the $20.00.

They are asked to describe the main character in the story. Half of the people described him as cold and uncaring, and half of the people described him as warm and genuine. The ones who responded that he was cold and uncaring, were the same strangers who were given iced coffee. Those who said he was warm and inviting, had been given warm coffee to hold.

You think you are aware of your thoughts and behaviors. But thirty minutes before these people were asked these questions, actors primed them.

We are being primed all day long by our environment. Advertisers, the media, and politicians are aware of these techniques. We are constantly being programmed, and yet we think we are actually in charge of our lives. We erroneously believe we are making our own decisions.

The only way to be in charge is to block out external sources and connect to yourself in the present moment.

Our thoughts create our reality. But it is really the beliefs that we have about the thoughts that manifest our world.

In order to change your reality, you can only do two things.

1. Change your beliefs, or
2. Change the definitions that we give to those beliefs/circumstances.

There are two diverse types of beliefs. Positive and negative. Positive beliefs are expansive and empowering. Negative beliefs restrict or limit us.

Want to know how to test if a belief is Positive or Negative? How does it make you feel?

Do you feel free? Expansive? Empowered? Excited?

Or do you feel sad, angry, restricted, unable to have what you desire?

Practice being aware of how you feel. This not only allows you to navigate the world easier, but it also builds trust in yourself. Trust in yourself builds confidence.

With positive beliefs, you will experience positive synchronicities.

With the negative, you will experience negative synchronicities.

For example, if you believe money is the root of all evil, and you win or inherit a large sum of money, you can potentially experience negative synchronicities that will reaffirm the negative belief you have about money such as a car breaking down, sickness, breakup, losing your job, etc. Because of the subconscious belief, anything you would attribute in your reality as 'negative' that occurs, you will consider as evidence to support the negative belief.

If you believe that all men are misogynist pigs, watch how quickly evidence will appear in your reality to confirm this. Your bestie will call you and tell you about a horrible date they went on. Your boss will start being a complete jerk to you. All the men you come in contact with will appear to conform to your belief.

Let's say that you believe a certain diet or workout will help you lose weight if you are consistent. You will lose weight.

If you believe you're the luckiest person in the world, you will see in your reality evidence that supports that. You'll win every raffle you ever buy. You'll always get the best parking spots, the best sales, the best discounts, and all that evidence will stack up and further impress on your subconscious that you are, in fact, the luckiest person in the world.

There is only one belief that is true. All other beliefs are limiting in some way shape or form. The only belief that is true is:

"I am."

"I am" is the true expression of who we are.

Positive beliefs empower us. They enable us to view the world as though we can CONQUER it. And the limiting ones, the negative beliefs, they hold us back. They LIMIT the Being that we are.

Now the trick is to smash the negative/limiting beliefs.

Most limiting beliefs, being fear based, have a trigger built into them.

A self-reinforcing trigger, says, I will die if I give up this belief.

The task is to become aware that we have limiting beliefs. Be aware that the natural response to letting it go will be fear or death.

Breathe light into it, embrace it, acknowledge it. Acknowledge that it exists, and it will continue to exist in the overall "I am."

"I am," equal to the universe and all that is.

The universe itself is "I am." It is everything.

The universe is all positive and negative aspects.

The universe is all positive beliefs and all negative beliefs.

existing as a whole. "I am," is infinite.

negative or limiting beliefs live on unless you create a circuit breaker.

To break a limiting belief, you initially acknowledge it and give it some love before introducing a more empowering belief to replace it.

The limiting belief will continue to live on in its own right but you don't need to follow it. You can choose to move forward believing something more empowering for yourself.

There is no need to take that negative belief and smash it. Simply identify it. Give it a kiss and choose to think a more powerful thought or belief.

Understanding how belief templates work, assists the process of choosing the ones that serve you.

Templates are, let us say, webs or honeycombs of beliefs that are strung together. You see this in religion, politics, spirituality. Sets of beliefs around the whole of society are evident. They are also held together by each other.

Let's examine two or more beliefs strung together. The more beliefs that are strung together, the further those belief structures and templates will be reinforced. They are built upon one another.

Templates become self-fulfilling prophecies. Really, all beliefs become self-fulfilling prophecies with which further perpetuate the belief systems. So the larger the template, the honeycomb, or the web, the deeper the belief system. The deeper the belief system, the deeper the resistance will be to let them go.

Another area to be aware of is our Reticular Activating System (RAS). This is a group of neurons in the base of the brain that filters data or information. Imagine though, that it is like the security guard of the brain. It filters out what is processed from your environment.

The brain can be exposed to over two million pieces of information a second. If you took that all in at once your brain would fry. Therefore, we programmed the RAS to take care of that processing. We tell the security guard at the gate what to pay attention to and what to ignore. This is achieved by what you FOCUS on.

Your RAS is only ever going to agree with you. You are always right. So whatever beliefs you have, it does not look for data or information to give you the actual truth. Your RAS goes on a search and seize mission to prove you are correct all of the time. It is constantly looking for evidence to support you. Now this security guard was programmed since birth. It was programmed by you, your caregivers, the people, and the society that you grew up in, so that those beliefs end up becoming yours.

Whatever you focus on, is what you will get.

It is what you are going to believe and allow in that is what will get filtered to you. Your RAS is going to gather evidence to support a belief you may have such as "all men are bad" or "all women are bad," 'money is evil," or "I cannot lose weight." Your RAS continually seeks out information to support what you are saying is true. It is a never-ending cycle. Your belief is constantly reinforced with more "evidence" that your belief is correct. And with that ongoing cycle occurring you never get anything different out of life.

The goal is to break these vicious cycles in your life, those repeating scenarios. Those same crappy relationships, money problems, weight diet problems and health problems, will continue until you break the pattern.

If you have a belief, regardless of whether it is positive or negative, it will lead you to a trail of evidence to further support that belief.

Let us say I have a positive belief that I am lovable. My RAS will be super hyper focused on finding supporting evidence that I am loved and that I am lovable, and it will just disregard any information that comes across my brain that suggests otherwise. That is positive synchronicity.

For the negative belief, let us say I am not lovable. My RAS will be super hyper focused on that belief. And we will be sifting and sorting through all of the information in my environment and only picking out the evidence that supports that I am not lovable. Any evidence that comes in that is contrary to your belief will firstly be ignored and filtered out. Or secondly, you will be repelled by it.

Remember the erroneous concept that I will die if I have to believe something else.

Ninety-five percent of our day is programmed early on in our day. Only 5% of our day is conscious behavior. This means you are only experiencing 5% of what your potential is.

Ninety-five percent of what can come to you is completely untapped. More love, abundance, more adventure, and vitality.

Our brain is like a computer. There are some points worth considering about the way it works.

1. Time is not linear.

2. The human brain only organizes time to appear that way when it is accessing information.

3. Everything exists now, in the present, and the present is the only thing that exists.

4. Every time you go to a memory – from your 'Past,' you open it, you download it into the Present moment. You are literally 'time' traveling or Quantum Jumping into a different timeline than the one you were currently in.

5. Your brain does not know the difference in time, or the difference between a real or imagined event. So, it is processing everything as actually happening in the PRESENT moment.

6. RAS will search out evidence to support your belief about that timeline.

7. Belief systems are self-reinforcing. They make you believe it is the only thing to believe.

What will you believe? You will want to define it and label it differently. Use it to your advantage - use permission slips.

A permission slip is an acknowledgement to yourself, an awareness of a certain limiting belief, and then permission for you to believe, think, act, etc. differently. These permissions are a great tool to use.

Your brain is a servo mechanism – meaning a machine you can control. Point it in the direction you want it to go in. What you focus on is what you get. Your State of Being (SOB) is how you feel. You want to direct your brain in the direction of what makes you FEEL good versus what makes you feel bad.

3 Things are important for DRIVING your SOB:

1. FOCUS

2. Self-Talk

3. Physiology

It is quite simple: FOCUS on what you want to feel good or FOCUS on what you do not want to feel bad. Your actions will align to this.

There will be more on this in Chapter 5, Values. But first let us explore our emotional vibrations and what we are putting out into the universe.

ACTIVITY:

1. Identify some beliefs you currently have about yourself that are "negative."

2. List the evidence you have gathered throughout your life that supports this belief.

3. What would you change about this belief - if you could?

CHAPTER 4

EMOTIONAL SCALE OF CONSCIOUSNESS AND OUR VIBRATIONAL ENERGY

"Be the energy you want to attract." —Buddha

"Stop trying to change the world since it is only the mirror. Man's attempt to change the world by force is as fruitless as breaking a mirror in the hope of changing his face. Leave the mirror and change your face. Leave the world alone and change your conceptions of yourself. The reflection then will be satisfactory."

— Neville Goddard, Your Faith is Your Fortune

"The universe is not outside of you. Look inside yourself; everything that you want, you already are." —Rumi

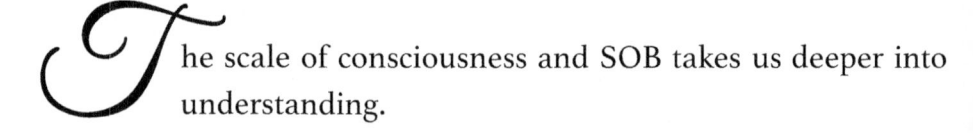

The scale of consciousness and SOB takes us deeper into understanding.

I initially studied the scale of consciousness by enjoying Dr. David R. Hawkins' book *Power versus Force*. I can highly recommend this amazing, incredible text. Dr. Hawkins describes our consciousness on a scale and I have adapted this to my coaching work in helping others to be who they want to be in life.

State of Being scale:

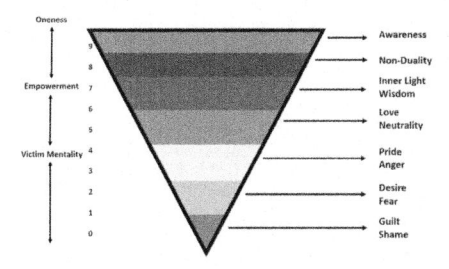

Scale of consciousness - State of Being aka SOB, determines the physical experience and makes your experience seem real. Physical reality is not real without the perceiver and their state.

I use this example on winning the lottery. Three people, three random people walk into a gas station and they each buy a scratch off lottery ticket. The first one wins $100, The second one wins $100, The third one wins $100. Their state of being though, is interesting. The first one, when they won, just act like it is a natural occurrence. The second one, jumps up and down, takes a picture of it - posts out on social media and is so excited. The third complains! They get angry! They needed to win $500. They are angry and disappointed.

Based on those three different scenarios, each of them won $100. Each of them responded a different way. Which one do you think has a life of abundance?

The person who just goes on and acts like it is natural is the one that brings in more abundance. They act as if it is a natural occurrence. Of course, naturally I won $100, and they go on about their day.

The person who jumps up and down, cheering for their success - we might think this person would naturally attract more abundance to be grateful for - but they don't. It was a shock to them. It was a surprise; it was something rare. They snapped out of a lack mentality for five seconds. Some random thing happened. The act of jumping up and down and celebrating in such a wild way, while not bad, is sending out to the universe - this is a shock. I cannot believe this. It communicates - I'm in lack - this cool thing just happened but it's not a normal thing in my life.

The third person is ungrateful. Stuck in a negative mindset of lack. They probably got home and had a $200 bill in the mail. Our State of Being determines the physical reality we experience. It also determines time. Time is perceived. If I am in a lower state of consciousness - State of Being time is going to drag. In the middle, it will "seem" normal. In a high state of consciousness or a high state of being - time is going to fly. Time flies when you are having fun.

Circumstances are an illusionary symbol, a reflection of your State of Being.

The Laws of creation state:

1. You exist

2. All is one

3. What you put out is what you get back

4. Everything changes except for the first three laws

It colors the experience and allows a unique perspective. Be playful. It allows things to be trans-mutable.

You will never get a one-on-one reflection immediately with the law of attraction. You want to be careful there is an echo that occurs. The first stage is the first reflection. It looks the same as it used to. It gives you an opportunity to respond in a different way to the circumstances. Even if they look the same. When you respond differently, then the response in the circumstances naturally and automatically change. The circumstances will change when you respond differently to the circumstances because you are different. You have transmuted the situation. This is a natural process and is already occurring in your life whenever we do things differently. We tend to create things the same out of habit and security, but you are already doing this change creation.

Therefore, there is no need to panic when these changes in circumstances start happening more obviously. It is like you are testing yourself. To see "is this the state that I wish to be in." "Is this the reality that I desire to be in." If you react to the circumstances, that communicates you are not ready. You have not changed in the particular area that you react to.

In quantum jumping, one can shift to five dimensional (5D) earth. Three dimensional (3D) can be victim mentality, it is fear based. There's a past, there is a future, everything is happening *to* me. I am the effect of my reality. In this way we are blaming life around us for making our circumstances. We aren't yet awake in consciousness to see we are in fact making it ourselves.

The next level, four dimensional (4D) is self-empowerment. Where love and neutrality exist. There is a present and a future and everything is happening *for* me. I am the cause of my reality. Next is 5D which is oneness.

Oneness. Unconditional Love. There is no time. Every single thing exists right here right now. I am everything. I am all that is. I am all reality. This is really important to contemplate and fully understand. It will empower you.

There are four levels in consciousness:

1. Physical consciousness is the lowest level of the mind.

2. Next is the Unconscious Mind - this is the part of the mind that does things automatically. I think of this as what the mind and body is programmed to do, based on the belief.

3. Then the subconscious is the third. This is the part of the mind that has programs running within, but we are unaware of those programs.

4. Lastly, the Higher Mind. Your imagination, which is the link between the physical mind and the Higher Mind.

Imagination is key to being connected to your Higher Self/Mind. It is how they communicate.

When we imagine the life we dream and desire our Higher Mind automatically translates that into being what we are actually doing and our circumstances begin to show up with aspects of those dreams in them. In this way our Higher Mind is available to us at all times and can inform and influence our day to day lives. Higher Mind shows us we have choices.

CHAPTER 4

There is a higher ego and a lower ego. Lower ego is that victim mentality.

You are the observer of the thoughts. You are tapped into the quantum field based on where you are standing. You attract the thoughts. This is the law of attraction. Circumstances do not matter, only state of being matters. Only your state of consciousness.

- If you are in a state of your lower ego, you are in a victim mentality. Everything is happening to you.

- In neutrality, everything is neutral. Everything is happening for me.

- In your higher mind, you are saying (and knowing), I am creating everything.

The key is to neutralize your ego so you can observe the reality you are creating and consciously choose the emotional response so you can consciously jump to a more preferred timeline.

If you are creating from the lower ego, the lower states of consciousness, you keep creating lack states or victim mentality or attachment. If you create from neutrality, you have no Fs to give about your circumstances. You are going to go with the flow, and experience time differently.

On the scale of consciousness, the ego exists only to observe the thoughts and circumstances. The only free will you have is deciding how you will interpret the circumstances that have already occurred and shifting your focus to your desired circumstances.

Based on that, you remember timelines that are available to you - from that state of consciousness. If you are in a victim mentality, neutrality, or love state of being.

If your state is coming from a victim mentality, you gather evidence from the past to support why you are not successful. This further perpetuates your victim mentality.

From the higher states you are gathering up evidence to support that everything will always work out for you. Tapping into timelines where solutions are possible, where success is inevitable.

You are not attracting anything except for the thoughts, and you are interpreting the thoughts based on the beliefs you have about yourself. Based on the beliefs, you forge new timelines based on the behaviors and actions you take.

The ego needs to come to a place of neutrality. Or it will continue to be in the victim mentality and pull in those same situations that match that victim frequency. Always. No exceptions. Unless you do something differently.

Want new circumstances? Let go. Everything is truly based on your current state. There's evidence to support all theories as Reality Transurfing suggests. (Vadim Zeland - Reality Transurfing)

The brain, the ego, is only ever the observer of thought.

CHAPTER 4

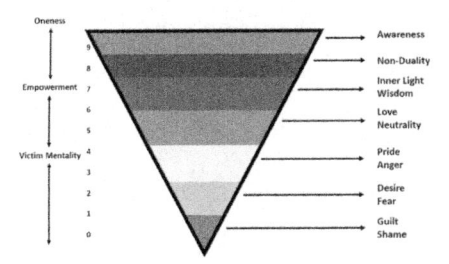

```
Oneness                                    Awareness
        9                                  Non-Duality
        8                                  Inner Light
Empowerment 7                              Wisdom
        6                                  Love
        5                                  Neutrality
Victim Mentality 4                         Pride
        3                                  Anger
        2                                  Desire
        1                                  Fear
        0                                  Guilt
                                           Shame
```

So, consider this scale from zero to let us say one thousand. Seven hundred and above is enlightenment.

Now I have taken his scale, and I have extrapolated it in a way that is helpful when I am coaching and helping others to access more enlightened states.

There are relationships to chakras.

The Root Chakra represents basic needs, water, shelter, food.

Regarding the base or root chakra you will notice some similarities in Maslow's hierarchy of Needs.

There is a lot that can be learned on the chakras and it is an advanced study so for now it's sufficient to understand the different states and levels. Down at the bottom we have the base or root chakra, then the sacral, the solar plexus, the heart, the throat, the third eye, and the crown chakra.

The Root Chakra can be understood in terms of responding to basic needs such as water, shelter, food.

There are a number of emotions associated with the chakra also. Those emotions are guilt, shame, apathy.

There are some positive interactions related to the base area such as sensual connection and so forth. Positive emotions are also added when combined with the heart chakra by being loving.

Okay, you can go up a little higher than that and you will experience desire. Fear is a little higher up the scale.

Above that, is pride and anger. Now anger is a higher state of consciousness than fear, guilt, shame, or apathy.

If I am in a state of depression, apathy, or guilt, it is in my best interest to get angry about something because that actually brings up my state of consciousness by activation. Apathy being no action or interest at all. Anger is at least active, thus raised from apathy.

Everything on the planet has consciousness. We can calibrate vibration or consciousness of everything. If we look at vegetables and fruits, they will have a higher state of vibrational consciousness than processed foods. If you look at classical music, it has a much higher consciousness or vibration than rap music. We can calibrate everything on this planet.

This lower calibration is what is called victim mentality. That vibration translates to everything happening against me. I am a victim in my reality. That is how I could experience lower levels of consciousness, guilt, shame, fear, or desire. If I am depressed, I am not feeling empowered. I am feeling like I am not in control of my environment. I am not feeling like I could get up and do anything to change my reality.

Now if I go to the next level in the middle, where love, neutrality, inner light, and wisdom are located, there are states of empowerment and neutrality. This translates to everything that is happening, *for* me. I feel empowered. Anything that happens in my life I feel confident that I can explore it and embrace those higher goals into my life. By using the world and its reflection as a mirror I can see what to tweak within myself ways to positively impact the reality that I am living in. This is empowerment. I feel empowered by experiencing life this way.

The lower level - victim mentality – is where we have the most limiting beliefs. Blaming others and having a victim mentality are the lower vibrational thoughts. They are the lowest beliefs that we could have about ourselves, completely restrained. Feeling like I do not have a lot of options. I am stuck here. I cannot move forward. The government has control of my life, feeling that my church has control over my life. Something other than me has control over my life. All of those kinds of thoughts.

When we get into the state of empowerment, I am not saying that I am in complete control of my life. I am saying that even if other things are happening around me, I can still take action. There are some things that I could still do to have a positive influence on my life, I feel more hopeful. I feel more empowered than at the lower level.

When you move up to the third level, the higher states of consciousness are there. Inner light, non-duality, and awareness. Non duality means there is no one else but me. I am. I am everything, I am all that exists. There are no other people in my reality. We are all One. There is no duality, there are no others. We are One. We are all the same being having different versions, different experiences in reality. We are all the same. There is nothing outside of me. That is a state of oneness.

This is the original state we have derived from. The oneness, all that is. The "I AM" of the universe. From there, based on our interpretation of events (beliefs and definitions), we will have different experiences.

It is the full "I am" and from that place, "I am" creating everything.

I am creating my reality. I am the creator of reality. I am the creator of my world. I am the Creator of the universe. I am the God of my reality.

It is important to take into consideration your state of being when you start to explore your thoughts and your beliefs. It is good to examine the definitions that you are giving to these.

Your state of being is the impetus that drives the thoughts that you have.

The thoughts that you have will drive the beliefs that you have. And the beliefs that you have will drive those definitions and vice versa.

Okay, consider it being like one big equation.

I am in a state of being where I am in guilt or shame, I only have access to other thoughts that will bring me guilt or shame.

If I am in a state of neutrality and my being is in neutrality, everything is neutral.

There is no causality.

There is no good or bad. There is no positive, there is no negative.

Everything just is.

CHAPTER 4

Everything is neutral. There is nothing happening against me. There is nothing happening for me. Everything just is. The only other thoughts that I have access to are neutral thoughts. I am not going to have access to guilt. I am not going to have access to other levels of thought.

My state of being will drive the thoughts that I have access to. The thoughts that I have access to, will then drive the beliefs. So, if I am down in fear, I am having thoughts of fear or I am having thoughts that make me afraid, it is going to trigger belief systems within me that will continuously bring up fear.

Like attracts like. If I am having depressed thoughts, I will have more depressed thoughts, unless I change my state of being. If I am angry, I will continuously have more anger unless I change my state of being.

If I feel loved, I will bring in more love unless I change my state of being. My state of being is the most important thing for me to be aware of.

There is a saying, "circumstances do not matter, only the state of being matters (Bashar)." Meaning, do not react to the 3D world. Do not react to your circumstances.

Do not allow your circumstances that are popping off in your reality to drive your state of being. Become aware of your state of being and drive your state of being yourself. Allow the circumstances to unfold to support your state of being. It has to match it if you hold firm with your state of being. Your reality will catch up and match its law. This is the law of attraction.

The most important job that you have is controlling your state of being. Again, your state of being drives your thoughts, which drives your beliefs and drives your definitions.

Now, all those things create feelings and feelings are what sends out the energy. That is the energy that is sent out into the universe. That is your vibration.

Your vibration sets your state of consciousness by what you are sending out into the universe. What your vibration sends such as your feelings of guilt, shame, pride, anger, love neutral is what will come back. Whatever goes out into the universe is what you will get back.

Our subconscious mind is running behind the scenes that we do not even know various programs are running.

It is interesting to know that 95% of what we are creating in our reality is from our subconscious. Our subconscious thoughts, beliefs, definitions that we are not aware that we have set in motion are running programs that influence our daily life.

We want to uncover the thoughts, the beliefs, the definitions and in order to do that we can look at the following:

1. Our emotions.

2. The mirror of our 3D reality. The people places and things that are showing up.

These are our navigational systems, our GPS to navigate our 3D reality.

The mirror also gives us the synchronicities, the positive or the negative synchronicities, to keep us moving along that path. That state of being, those thoughts, those beliefs, and those definitions to which you are aligned.

When you change your state of being, your state of consciousness or awareness changes. When you are in the higher state, focus on what you are feeling in the moment, and purposely focus it towards the direction that you want, from here you will gain the outcome that you had in mind.

That is how you change your reality.

ACTIVITY:

1. Identify the TOP 5 emotions you feel on a daily basis.

2. Identify the % of time you are in that state.

3. Where do you fit on the Scale? Is it possible to imagine that your reality is based on your State of Being? That your circumstances are driven by the feelings you have on a daily basis?

4. Identify how you would prefer to feel every day.

CHAPTER 5

HIERARCHY OF NEEDS

"Every intention sets energy into motion, whether you are aware of it or not." —Henry David Thoreau

"You create your own universe as you go along." —Winston Churchill

"Dare to believe in the reality of your assumption and watch the world play its part relative to its fulfillment." — Neville Goddard

---

Understanding our needs as humans is critical to understanding why we do things, especially at a subconscious level. The more you begin to understand why you behave the way you do, the faster you can address it and the easier it will be to reprogram your behaviors to optimize your life.

CHAPTER 5

Maslow's Needs: https://canadacollege.edu/dreamers/docs/Maslows-Hierarchy-of-Needs.pdf

Maslow's hierarchy of needs is a theory of motivation which identifies five categories of human needs which dictate our behaviors.

They are:

1. Physiological Needs – things like food, water, warmth, rest
2. Safety Needs – security and safety, shelter, and protection
3. Belongingness and Love Needs – Intimate relationships, family, friends
4. Esteem Needs – prestige and feelings of accomplishment
5. Self-Actualization. - achieving one's full potential, including creative activities

The lower needs must be fulfilled before moving up to the next level. See below.

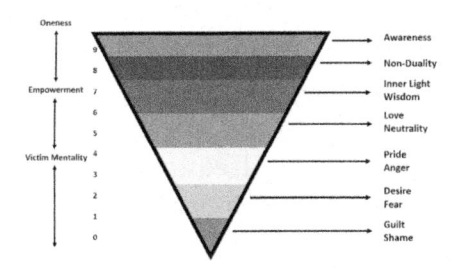

The five stages can be identified as deficiency or growth stages.

The lower – are deficiency driven. As the need is unmet, and the longer a person is deficient – they will be MORE motivated to get it met. Once a need is met, we can more easily move on to the next need to get that one met. Not everyone moves straight up, some shift up and down depending on life's circumstances. Not everyone reaches the self-actualized or Growth level of needs in their lifetime.

What needs do you have that are being met and what needs are you looking to get met?

There are certain needs that you may want to have met that are not being met now.

Ask yourself, what are some of the habits that could be put in place to meet those needs for yourself. This is about choosing the right habits to support the needs that you want to have met.

It is an ongoing quest to reach one's full potential. As a person reaches the summit of Maslow's motivation theory it is not an end point. Unlike lower-level needs, this higher need is never fully satisfied as one grows psychologically. There are always new opportunities to grow self-actualized people tend to have motivators such as truth, justice, wisdom and meaning.

Self-actualized people have frequent occurrences of peak experiences which are described as energized moments of profound happiness and harmony.

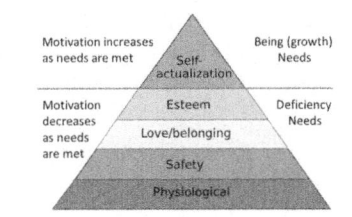

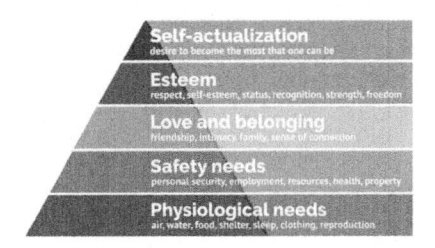

This was later expanded to include transcendence, cognitive and aesthetic needs.

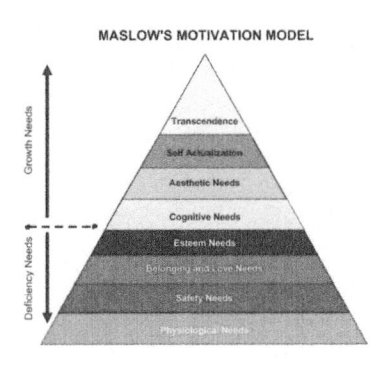

ACTIVITY: For each of the Needs, identify how you are currently getting these met and then identify new ways you can have them met.

Hierarchy of Needs	Definition	How you currently meet these:	New ways for you to meet these needs:
Physiological Needs	Basic human needs such as water, food, shelter, comfort, etc.		
Safety Needs	The desire for security, stability, and safety		
Social Needs	The desire for affiliation including friendship and belonging		
Esteem Needs	The desire for self-respect, and respect from others		
Self-Actualization	The desire for self-fulfillment		

Needs List

CONNECTION

Security

Equality

Consciousness

Acceptance

Stability

Harmony

Contribution

Affection

Support

Inspiration

Creativity

Appreciation

To Know

Order

Discovery

Belonging

To Be Known

PHYSICAL WELLBEING

Efficacy

Cooperation

To See

Air

Effectiveness

Communication

To Be Seen

Food

Growth

Closeness

To Understand

Movement

Hope

Community

To Be Understood

Exercise

Learning

Companionship

Trust

Rest/Sleep

Mourning

Compassion

Warmth

Sexual Expression

Participation

Consideration

HONESTY

Safety

Purpose

Consistency

Authenticity

Shelter

Self-Expression

Empathy

Integrity

Touch

Stimulation

Inclusion

Presence

Water

To Matter

Intimacy

PLAY

MEANING

Understanding

Love

Joy

Awareness

AUTONOMY

Mutuality

Humor

Celebration of life

Choice

Nurturing

PEACE

Challenge

Freedom

Respect/Self-Respect

Beauty

Clarity

Independence

Safety

Communion

Competence

Space

Ease

Spontaneity

How We Feel When Our Needs Are Met:

AFFECTIONATE

Ardent

Delighted

Stimulated

Compassionate

Aroused

Glad

INSPIRED

Friendly

Astonished

Happy

Amazed

Loving

Dazzled

Jubilant

Awed

Open hearted

Eager

Pleased

Wonder

Sympathetic

Energetic

Tickled

EXCITED

Tender

Enthusiastic

PEACEFUL

Amazed

Warm

Giddy

Calm

Animated

CONFIDENT

Invigorated

Clear headed

Thankful

Empowered

Lively

Comfortable

Touched

Open

Passionate

Centered

HOPEFUL

Proud

Surprised

Content

Expectant

Safe

Vibrant

Equanimity

Encouraged

ENGAGED

EXHILARATED

Fulfilled

Optimistic

Absorbed

Blissful

Mellow

JOYFUL

Alert

Ecstatic

Peace

Amused

Curious

Elated

Quiet

Enlivened

Engrossed

Enthralled

Relaxed

Reinvigorated

Enchanted

Exuberant

Relieved

Rejuvenated

Entranced

Radiant

Satisfied

Renewed

Fascinated

Rapturous

Serene

Rested

Interested

Thrilled

Still

Restored

Intrigued

GRATEFUL

Tranquil

Revived

Involved

Appreciative

Trusting

Spellbound

Moved

REFRESHED

Feelings When Our Needs aren't Satisfied:

AFRAID

Hostile

Turbulent

Despair

Apprehensive

Repulsed

Turmoil;

Despondent

Dread

CONFUSED

Uncomfortable

Disappointed

Foreboding

Ambivalent

Uneasy

Discouraged

Frightened

Baffled

Unnerved

Disheartened

Mistrustful

Bewildered

Unsettled

Forlorn

Panicked

Dazed

Upset

Gloomy

Petrified

Flummoxed

EMBARRASSED

Heavy Hearted

Scared

Hesitant

Ashamed

Hopeless

Suspicious

Lost

Chagrined

Melancholy

Terrified

Mystified

Flustered

Mournful

Wary

Perplexed

Guilty

Unhappy

Worried

Puzzled

Mortified

Wretched

ANNOYED

Torn

Self-Conscious

TENSE

Aggravated

DISCONNECTED

Fatigue

Anxious

Dismayed

Alienated

Beat

Cranky

Disgruntled

Aloof

Burnt Out

Distressed

Displeased

Apathetic

Depleted

Distraught

Exasperated

Bored

Exhausted

Edgy

Frustrated

Cold

Lethargic

Fidgety

Impatient

Detached

Listless

Frazzled

Irritated

Distant

Sleepy

Irritable

Irked

Distracted

Tired

Jittery

ANGRY

Indifferent

Weary

Nervous

Enraged

Numb

Worn Out

Overwhelmed

CHAPTER 5

Furious

Removed

PAIN

Restless

Incensed

Uninterred

Agony

Stressed Out

Indignant

Withdrawn

Anguished

VULNERABLE

Urate

DISQUIET

Bereaved

Fragile

Livid

Agitated

Devastated

Guarded

Outraged

Alarmed

Grief

Helpless

Resentful

Disconcerted

Heartbroken

Insecure

AVERSION

Disturbed

Hurt

Leery

Animosity

Perturbed

Lonely

Reserved

Appalled

Rattled

Miserable

Sensitive

Contempt

Restless

Regretful

Shaky

Disgusted

Shocked

Remorseful

YEARNING

Dislike

Startled

SAD

Envious

Hate

Surprised

Depressed

Jealous

Horrified

Troubled

Dejected

Longing

ACTIVITY:

1. Identify the top needs you get met consistently.

2. Identify the top needs you want to get met consistently.

3. What strategy have you used in the past to get your needs met?

4. Is there anything you would change about those strategies?

CHAPTER 6

VALUES AND INTENTION

"You already have within you everything you need to turn your dreams into reality." — Wallace D. Wattles

"You become what you think about most, but you also attract what you think about most." — John Assaraf

"Change your conception of yourself and you will automatically change the world in which you live. Do not try to change people; they are only messengers telling you who you are. Revalue yourself and they will confirm the change."

— Neville Goddard, Your Faith is Your Fortune

What do you want?

Most people are not even aware of what they really want, what their true heart's desire is. They have been told their whole life, who to be and what to do. That their dreams are not possible and to forget about them. So they lack confidence or trust in themselves to live out their dreams or to follow through on their goals and desires. They are afraid to even acknowledge what they want. They are afraid of judgment. They are afraid their family will not support them, or people in general will not support them. Many fear their particular needs or higher goals will not get met – so they stay quiet and small.

We can sabotage or procrastinate when our desires or values appear not to align with our current reality.

The following exercise in understanding what your TRUE VALUES are was enlightening for me. Not only did it solidify in my mind what was important to me, but it helped me identify why I keep sabotaging myself and my success! It helped me identify why I kept sabotaging the very things that I had said that I really wanted.

We can also sabotage or procrastinate when our desires appear to be competing with how our life is evolving. This was the case for me, mine were competing. Meaning I've placed 1 or more values above others and if those top values are threatened, I'll sacrifice or sabotage the lower one, to keep my higher values.

There are two reasons why we are motivated to do things, one is reward and the second is to avoid pain.

So, if you are sabotaging you must ask yourself this question. What is causing this? Why am I sabotaging? Why am I procrastinating?

Do I get a reward by not doing something? Is this purely a habit? Or is there some reward that I am getting from my current circumstances staying as they are?

What pain might I be avoiding by procrastinating or continuing with this habit?

Now with sabotage, there are four main factors why we sabotage ourselves.

1. Low self-concept

2. Internalized beliefs

3. Fear of the unknown

4. Excessive need for control

Here is how you can figure this out. The following exercise can show you what applies to you.

Exercise:

Sit down with a blank piece of paper. Clear your mind and imagine this.

You have just been everything that you ever wanted right here right now. How do you feel?

Write down the top ten feelings quickly.

Do not overthink this, jot down the top ten feelings or at least the top five feelings that you feel.

You have everything that you ever desired, you have everything that you ever dreamed of.

How do you feel? Next, take the top three feelings. Place them in hierarchical order.

So, one being the most important, then two and then three.

I had a huge epiphany when I did this. In minutes I became aware that I had competing values. And as I started to get my needs met in one of my top values, I saw how it began to threaten my top value. Therefore, I would sabotage or procrastinate.

We do this because our minds, our bodies, 'think' they must bring us back into safety - into homeostasis. Our subconscious is programmed to do that. The self-sabotaging behavior, the procrastination is exactly how our brains are designed to protect us to keep us safe. Those behaviors are PROTECTING us. Once you are aware that procrastination and sabotage are like a defense mechanism that is built into our subconscious to keep us safe, then you can become friends with it.

So, my top values at the time were peace, security, and freedom. I was just starting out in my business, and initially I did not understand why I kept sabotaging or procrastinating. After completing this exercise, I had great insights into what was occurring. I realized that as soon as my financial security started to increase and I had more income, I sabotaged that by slacking off. I was building a business that was building more financial security, more stability in my life. This was where I would continue to be in control myself. Versus working for someone else who had control over me as a boss.

Instead of slacking off, that is the point where more energy should be utilized to drive forward and take more action. But instead of taking more inspired action I started to slow down.

One of my most important values in life was being challenged and competed with. I came to realize that my top value was peace and that more business, more work was going to disrupt my peace.

Even though increased income was going to bring me security, that value of security was only my number two. My top priority was peace. It was the most important to me because most of my life was chaotic.

Values can be the things that we desire. How we want to feel today is usually a result of what we did not have. Our needs or wants are attempting to fill a lack. They are based on the experiences from our past.

Peace is my top value. It became my number one due to my past having been very chaotic. Now that I had created a life of peace, anything that I perceived to threaten that I would sabotage. I also noticed this with romantic relationships. Anytime I had a person come into my life, that it was adventurous, or if there was a lot of security around the relationship, I began to sabotage it. I had a belief that romantic relationships would be chaotic because that was my past experience and if I thought it may threaten my peace, I simply wasn't going to allow that my subconscious was programmed to sabotage those connections, to take care of keeping me safe. To stay where I was getting other values met.

It was not until I began to imagine and work on affirmations that I realized that I could have peace, security, freedom, and adventure. All those things can exist in a co-existing reality. I could live without chaos, without insecurity.

Once I was able to picture a timeline where all those things could exist at the same time things started to take off. I stopped procrastinating, I stopped sabotaging.

Most people are not aware of why they are sabotaging or procrastinating. It is because they have erroneous beliefs that their values are competing with the way they want life to be. Once a threat comes along a fear enters believing that those values will not get met. But it doesn't have to be this way.

There is a situation that occurs with some men. I know a lot of men who value freedom over everything else. They may meet someone; they may even fall in love with someone. But because freedom is their top value, they may have a belief that being in a committed relationship will threaten their freedom. They believe they will no longer be free. Therefore, they tend to sabotage that connection.

Even if they want to be in a committed relationship, even if they are in love with someone, they will still sabotage that connection. That is, if that top value that they hold appears to be threatened, their subconscious will move in to protect it. Most people are not even aware that this is what is happening in relationships. It is a subconscious thing.

Values drive our identity. Identity drives our behavior.

Once you define your values they become your identity, which becomes your behavior. So the value you want the most, or the need for it drives your behavior. So you can see if your needs are not being met. It drives your behavior too.

The conflicts and the things that we would change about ourselves, or the things that we get upset about ourselves like why we procrastinate, and self-sabotage are because there are competing values.

If your values, the things that are important to you do not line up with Society's values, you will have conflict. I felt this conflict when I went through my "awakening" several years ago.

Once I decided I would BE who I wanted to be, I found that I had to move away from the people I grew up with. I could not be free to be who I wanted to be as they did not support my goals and dreams. More importantly, I needed to find out WHO I wanted to be but could not do that in the same environment that created the scared little girl I had become. So, I moved.

Decide what your values are and what's the most important to you. Discover what are your top five to ten core values. Define what they mean for you to have them as central in your life. And then let all the others go. Define and refine until you have identified only the things that are important to you. Tell yourself you are not going to compromise on them for other values. You are not going to judge yourself and that you are not going to allow society to browbeat you. Because those are your values. Reassure yourself that even though they may not appear to be in alignment with society's, your family or friend's views of what you should do, that you are going for it.

In coaching, I see a lot of couples realizing that their values do not align. It is why they cannot seem to get along or be on the same page. This is something we as adults need to learn and understand about ourselves. And we need to teach our children to identify their values too and encourage them to seek out friends and partners who align with those values.

The following activity helps to align yourself without competing beliefs.

ACTIVITY:

1. Identify your top values.
2. Identify ways/strategies you currently meet/attempt to meet them.
3. Identify ways they may be competing against each other.
4. Create a slide or a little movie in your head where all your needs and values are being met simultaneously. As you begin to work with this image, see the resistance slip away.

This works. You will start to procrastinate or sabotage less and less. In fact, when you begin to sabotage or procrastinate in daily life, you will recall that this is a defense mechanism, and you will be able to make the choice to move forward or pull back. Being conscious of your behavior is key. Being open and honest with yourself is imperative.

Once you have identified your values and how you will get your needs met, it is time to set intentions. People usually just set an intention and fail to link this with what they really want to achieve. They really want to have their needs and values met. So, by planning and setting an intention this acts as a springboard to action. Intention means – a plan or what you intend to do. In the back of this book, you will find a worksheet where you can begin building this type of plan for yourself. The plan will consist of what you really desire and how you will go about achieving it.

Do not worry about how you will achieve it yet. Once you read this book in its entirety, you will have begun building the confidence you need to execute your plan!

CHAPTER 6

CHAPTER 7

SELF CONCEPT AND IDENTITY

"We must radiate success before it will come to us. We must become mentally, from an attitude standpoint, the people we wish to become." —Earl Nightingale

"The more you praise and celebrate your life, the more there is in life to celebrate." —Oprah Winfrey

"You manifest what you believe, not what you want." —Sonia Ricotti

Self-concept is how I perceive myself. The concept of myself. My identity. My Ego self. The avatar I play in this lifetime.

We get this concept of ourselves from a few various places.

1. A high percentage of our self-concept comes from others, and the communication from others or the feedback that we get from them.

2. Self-observation - how we observe ourselves, what we observe about ourselves, our self-awareness.

3. Group association – Identifying with a group and their identity/behaviors. i.e., If you are a Catholic, a Protestant, Republican or Liberal, or a Steelers fan, etc. we get our self-concept from these group associations.

4. Assumed roles – mom, dad, sister, teacher, coworker, etc. These are roles which are assigned to us based on relationships.

5. Lastly, are social comparisons, where you compare yourself with those in your society and social circles. This one is a little complex…. there is an upward comparison and a downward comparison. So, depending on where you are in reality, you could be looking upward like oh, I want to be a multi-millionaire, multi billionaire or you could be looking downward at people, I don't want to be poor like my parents, friends, siblings.

Self-concept is also the set self-image. When we make changes at this level, it impacts the outer world or reflects in the outer world. Our self-image is buried in our subconscious.

What you believe about yourself in the subconscious, is reflected in the 3D world. Who do you believe you are?

Whoever you believe yourself to be is true and will be reflected in your outer world.

Your Self-Concept is the story you tell yourself, about you. That story is LIMITED based on the beliefs you have taken on over the course of your life. Remember, you are all that is. You are the Universe. You are the "I AM." Anything less than that is limiting.

Over the course of my life, I told a story that I was a victim. A victim of child abuse, a victim of domestic violence, a victim of narcissists that just kept showing up in my reality. I was constantly questioning my sanity. I was also, subconsciously believing that I deserved to be treated this way.

Remember, at 5 years old I was told by an important person in my church, good things happen to good people, bad things happen to bad people. Therefore, I must be a TERRIBLE person.

It was not until I began peeling away the limiting beliefs I had about myself, that I realized I had become a self-fulfilling prophecy. My thoughts, my beliefs and how I felt about myself, the story I kept telling me, about me, was what was creating my reality, further perpetuating my pain and suffering.

Since improving my Self- Concept, I no longer come in contact with narcissistic people.

Let us do an experiment. Let us say you are wearing a blue shirt. And I walk up to you and tell you I hate red shirts. How do you feel about that? You do not feel any way about it. In fact, you probably think I am crazy. You would not be insulted or upset because IT HAS NOTHING to do with you. You are not wearing a red shirt; it does not apply to you.

What if I walked up to you and told you that you were lazy or stupid? You would not react to it IF YOU DIDN'T believe it about yourself. You would walk away, thinking I was insane. But what if you had a subconscious fear or belief that you were lazy or stupid? How would you react? You would get sucked right into my delusion.

The world is a mirror of what we believe about ourselves. It takes practice and detachment to look into the mirror and identify your limiting beliefs.

Can you identify your negative self-concept?

Do you believe you are a person who gets cheated on all the time?

Do you believe you are a person who gets ghosted?

Do you believe you are a person who will never get ahead in life?

These are just beliefs. They are not facts. They are not truths. They will come true if you continue to tell that story.

Whatever you assume about you and your reality, will manifest.

Beliefs = Assumptions.

We act out what we believe to be true of ourselves.

• If I believe/assume the rich get richer, and there is no hope for the rest of us, I will not take steps to learn how to make more money. I will not take risks, investing my money.

• If I believe/assume I am always cheated on, I will always be suspicious of the person I am talking to/dating. I will never truly trust them. I will sneak around, trying to catch them. I will accuse them of misdemeanors. I will keep my thinking to myself; I will not be honest and open. I will be quite toxic for sure. What do you think manifests when you are showing up in a relationship like this?

- If I am a person who gets ghosted or love bombed early on, only to be abandoned, what type of behaviors will I exhibit in the connection? They certainly will not be healthy.

- If I am an open, affectionate, lovable person who always attracts great people in my life, what kind of behaviors will I consistently show?

- If I am the hardest working, most successful person at my job, I have no problem initiating a conversation with my boss about a promotion or a raise. If I do not feel this way about myself, I will never approach my boss.

- If I believe I have trustworthy people around me at all times, when they ask me for something or to invest in a business deal, I logically decide if it's the right course for me. If people are always out to cheat me, I will not even consider the investment, even if it is guaranteed to succeed.

My behavior is driven by my beliefs and assumptions.

My actions are driven by my identity.

The direction of my entire life is driven by my concept of self.

Therefore, any positive change to self-concept, improves the direction of my life. No exceptions.

In James Clear's book, *Atomic Habits*, (highly recommend this book), he introduces Tiny Gains. The concept of changing your life, 1% every day, has a compounding positive impact of 37.78% in 1 year.

Imagine your life today getting 30-40% better in 1 year.

CHAPTER 7

Why wouldn't you make small incremental changes then?

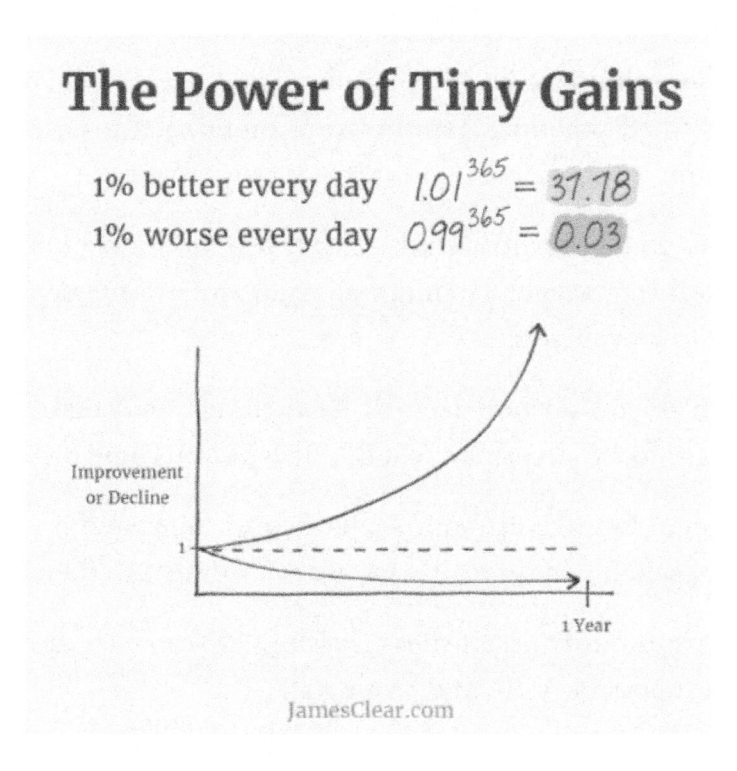

The Power of Tiny Gains

1% better every day $1.01^{365} = 37.78$
1% worse every day $0.99^{365} = 0.03$

Improvement or Decline

1 Year

JamesClear.com

You will FEEL a negative feeling, when there is a conflict between what you perceive about yourself and what your higher self KNOWS about you. Those negative emotions that you feel when you are rejected, ghosted, fired, lied to.... that awful feeling you get is your higher self, telling you NOT to believe those negative things about yourself!

Your higher self knows that you are everything.

When you are born, you are merged with your higher self.

You are all that is and as you are moving along and bumping through life Your caregiver's, society, and the people around you are telling you how to be in the world. They are shaping who you are and who you should be. And your self-concept begins to shrink.

Your higher self is layered with templates and beliefs. Laid on top of your unlimited potential, limiting you. Limiting the 'I AM' being that you are.

Therefore, you begin to shrink. Think less of yourself. You start carrying all this weight around, believing you are messed up and you need to fix yourself.

The truth is you do not need to fix a thing. You need to STOP TRYING to "fix" yourself and just BE. Be who you came here to be.

As you begin to wake up, your avatar begins to expand. Expand its concept of self. Begins to realize we are everything. All that is.

As we expand our consciousness is rising. We can then bring forth our highest possible self - that is our goal.

ACTIVITY:

1. Identify your current beliefs about an aspect of your life. Pick one aspect below.

- Career
- Finance
- Health/Wellness
- Relationships
- Romantic Relationships

Brainstorm every belief you have about that subject/aspect.

2. Identify the negative or limiting beliefs.

3. Identify the beliefs that aspect has towards you. For instance, if this is for your career, identify all the reasons your employer won't promote you, or pays you little money. Identify what you BELIEVE is the reason you don't have what you want.

4. Take all of the negative beliefs and write out positive affirmations to counter these beliefs.

CHAPTER 8

SELF CONFIDENCE AND TRUST

"Whatever you can do, or dream you can, begin it. Boldness has genius, power, and magic in it. Begin it now." —Johann Wolfgang von Goethe

"You are the creator of your own reality." —Esther Hicks

"Once you replace negative thoughts with positive ones, you'll start having positive results." —Willie Nelson

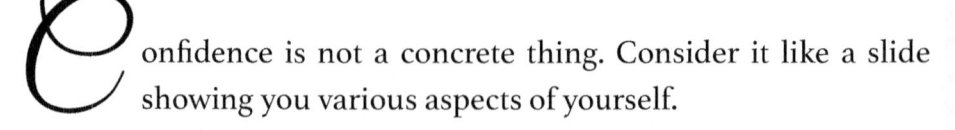

Confidence is not a concrete thing. Consider it like a slide showing you various aspects of yourself.

I can be confident in my success or assured of my failure. Or it could be somewhere in between - in the middle. It is going to depend on the subject or the situation. Certain things I am noticeably confident in other things I am not as confident with.

How do you build confidence? How do you learn how to trust again? Confidence comes from a trust in oneself that you will be able to deal physically and mentally with whatever happens in life. It comes from taking accountability for your life. Being responsible for how you see things in your life and no one else's. How you make things happen in life is your responsibility alone.

When you take responsibility, you are making a commitment. Everything that happens moving forward, is clearly seen as directly coming from your own decisions or actions. You realize that you will deal with the circumstances and the consequences of your actions.

The more I learned to trust myself and take responsibility for my life. The more confident I became.

In Napoleon Hill's book *Think and Grow Rich,* he has an excellent Self-Confidence Formula. I have used this for several years now and the Definite Chief Aim. The Self-Confidence formula is a contract with yourself. It is a tool to merge you back with yourself, re-build trust in yourself.

I know that I have the ability to achieve the object of my definite purpose in life.

Therefore, I demand of myself persistent continuous action towards its attainment. And I hear now promise to render such action.

I realized the dominating thoughts of my mind will eventually reproduce themselves in outward physical action and gradually transform themselves into physical reality.

Therefore, I will concentrate my thoughts for 30 minutes daily, upon the task of thinking of the person I intend to become. Thereby creating a clear mental picture of that person. I know that the principle of auto suggestion of any desire that I persistently hold in my mind will eventually seek expression through some practical means of attaining the focused object.

Therefore, I will devote 10 minutes daily to demanding of myself the development of self-confidence.

I have clearly written down a description of my definite chief aim in life, and I will never stop trying.

Until I have developed sufficient self-confidence for its attainment, I fully realized that no wealth or position can long endure unless built upon truth and justice. Therefore, I will engage in no transaction which does not benefit all whom it affects. I will succeed by attracting to myself the forces I wish to use and the cooperation of other people.

I will induce others to serve me because of my willingness to serve others. I will eliminate hatred, envy, jealousy, selfishness, and cynicism, by developing love for all humanity. Because I know that a negative attitude towards others can never bring me success. I will cause others to believe in me, because I will believe in them and in myself.

I will sign my name to this formula committed to memory and repeated a loud once a day with full faith that I will gradually influence my thoughts and actions, so that I will become a self-reliant and successful person. (Napoleon Hill in *Think and Grow Rich,* published 1937. p. 52-3)

Make this commitment to yourself: sign and date the document. Repeat this self-confidence formula on a daily basis. The amount of self confidence and trust I've built in myself, has significantly increased since I began using it.

Confidence is built with trust. Trust in self. In that document, I have laid out the promise to myself, and made a contract to myself that I will never stop. I will never stop until I achieve what I set out to do.

I will never give up on myself. I will never give up on my dreams. And it is with this type of determination that builds your confidence.

If you know beyond any doubt that from now until the day you die, you will work on something until you solve it, until you attain it, until you receive it.

Every day when you wake up there will be a fire lit within you.

Self-confidence is about trust.

Trusting yourself to keep going, to keep moving. To get back up no matter how many times you are knocked down. To move in a different direction. If you fail, you get up and you take another action, you take a different action, you re-strategize.

You never stop.

That is how you build confidence.

That is how I can walk into any room and know that I will not fail. I will never ever fail.

I may have small setbacks, but I will not fail because I will never give up. I trust myself that I will never give up.

I trust that I will always manage the situation correctly. I trust that if I do not know how to manage the situation, I will ask someone. I will admit that I do not know the answer.

Trust is the cornerstone of the foundation that you are building and trust in yourself.

This is how you build confidence, that is how you become successful.

That is the formula.

ACTIVITY:

1. Identify the top 3-5 goals you want to achieve.

2. Write/Type your Self-confidence formula.

3. Post your goals and Self-Confidence formula all over your home and office.

4. Read it daily.

5. I record mine along with my affirmations and play it several times throughout the day.

CHAPTER 9

BRIDGE OF INCIDENTS

"What you radiate outward in your thoughts, feelings, mental pictures and words, you attract into your life." —Catherine Ponder

"Your whole life is a manifestation of the thoughts that go on in your head." —Lisa Nihols

"Chance or accident is not responsible for the things that happen to you, nor is predestined fate the author of your fortune or misfortune.

Your subconscious impressions determine the conditions of your world. The subconscious is not selective; it is impersonal and holds no differentiation of persons. The subconscious is not concerned with the truth or falsity of your feelings. It always accepts as true that which you feel to be true. Feeling is the assent of the subconscious to the truth of that which is declared to be true.

Because of this quality of the subconscious there is nothing impossible to man. Whatever the mind of man can conceive and feel as true, the subconscious can and must objectify. Your feelings create the pattern from which your world is fashioned, and a change of feeling is a change of pattern."

—Neville Goddard, Resurrection

In order to fully understand the bridge of incidents that occurs, we must understand synchronicities. There are two types of synchronicities, positive and negative. Depending on what you are focused on, have been focused on the unwanted then you will see negative synchronicities. If you have been focused on the positive things that you want, you will see positive synchronicities. You receive synchronicities to give you a green light to move forward and a red light that you cannot go no further, this is not your path.

This concept was first introduced by Carl Jung. He described synchronicity as a casual, connecting principle, in which events both large and small in the external world might align to the experience of the individual, mirroring or echoing personal concerns or thoughts.

Synchronicity is a Greek word defined by Carl Jung In the 1950s.

SYN means together. CHRON means Khronos. Khronos means time.

Uncanny coincidences that seem to string meaningful things together, sewing the fabric, the bridge between space and time.

CHAPTER 9

Momentum, the quantity of motion in physics. This is space travel having a moving body of matter in 3d, measured as a product of its mass plus velocity.

It is matter in 3D and the time that it takes to travel through space. The impetus gained here by a moving object speeding up of an object in the time space continuum.

The speed of light time synchronizes. Einstein's theory of special relativity says time slows down or speeds up depending on how fast you move through space. The theory of general relativity space and time are the same entity. They are not separate.

The old saying "Time flies when you are having fun," is jumping through parallel realities all day long, 24/7. The synchronicities and momentum builds. Time seems to speed up when you jump to that reality. The space is necessary, so you are shown a different perspective to shift into the reality that you prefer. circumstances do not matter, only state of being matters.

1. Regarding circumstances - there is no past, present and future, they do not exist in any of those realities.
2. Stop playing a victim - Remember the scale of consciousness.
3. Forgive - use the Ho'oponopono method.
4. Use my quantum jumping meditations.
5. Accept that you created the current version of you, and commit to creating a new one.
6. Let go of the old timeline - this will help you move faster into the new timeline.

With time, if you are following your highest joy, then you have enough time to do what it is that you need to do. Your excitement comes in the form of synchronicities. You want to act on those. It shows you what you need to do.

There is an organizing principle - let synchronicity be your guide. You do not need to do all the other things you 'think' you need to do... you need to just trust.

Worrying tends to make you miss things. Things seem to accelerate and it feels like you are not managing in the moment. Instead of worrying, take it easy and do more with less time. We are actually creating time.

Our societal definitions of time are not accurate. You do not need more time unless you create more crap that you think you need to do.

You always get what you need. If you are living in the moment, it is a springboard to a more positive reality. Wanting creates polarization and resistance. Instead, use preferences, choose whatever you prefer.

I had a personal experience that illustrates this. In July 2017, I was going through my cancer treatment. And a friend of mine had a jeep and was posting all these awesome adventures with pictures of Jeep excursions. I kept thinking oh, I really want to get a Jeep. I was heavily in debt plus I was sick. There is no way that I could have bought a jeep.

As I got the thought that I wanted the Jeep, I knew it represented adventure, a life after cancer. What I did was simply focus on some point in the future. I told myself I am going to have a Jeep and I am going to go on lots of adventures. Something positive for me to look forward to.

Fast forward nine months. I am in more debt with medical bills. I am finishing my treatments. And I am sitting in the hospital having a treatment one particular day. And some random number pops up on my phone and I normally would not answer my phone if I do not know who it is.

I did answer the phone and it was a car dealership, a Jeep dealership. They said hey, several months ago you filled out an online enquiry. I did not remember doing this. They said that you were interested in a certain type of Jeep of a certain color and style and we have the exact Jeep here that you are looking for. And I said "Well, I am not really in a position to buy anything", and they said, "Well why don't you just stop down and take a look at it". So, I thought what the heck. I had nothing else going on that day. I figured go take it for a ride, have some fun and go home. I went down. It was the exact Jeep that I wanted the exact color. It had very low miles on it and had been garaged. It looked absolutely brand new. And I asked the guy how much it was, I discovered I could afford it.

And he invites me in to sit down. So, we were chit chatting. And the next thing I know I ended up driving off the lot with the Jeep.

The crazy thing is I was leasing a car at the time I was only like a year in of a three-year lease. So, I expected that if I got rid of the lease, I would have to pay a ton of money. And I could not really afford the payments of a new Jeep and I did not even think I was going to get approved for a loan because my credit was so bad.

At some point during the conversation, I realized that this salesperson was actually the manifestation that I was looking for. I had this sense that the universe set up the whole thing to make the Jeep mine and His manifestation happened.

I drove home with the jeep. I actually got approved for it. I do not know how I made the payments, but I got the other car lease taken care of. It all just worked out. and when I went there, I was just neutral like yes, let me just take it for a ride. See what it is like. This is really cool. I wasn't even super excited; I was calm and neutral about the whole thing. And how it all unfolded to this day still blows my mind.

The problem though, is that most of us are not aware of our beliefs or the mental chatter that goes on in our head. We are not aware of some of our beliefs that are holding us back from having everything that we desire. So how do we counteract these? We use affirmations, affirmations or I am statements that affirm the beliefs we want to impress upon the mind or the subconscious. I use I am statements for example. I am financially secure. I became a millionaire overnight. I am.

I have multiple streams of passive income; my wealth doubles every day. It is important to place emphasis on these types of thoughts when visualizing the dream life you want. And use your heart and mind coordination.

Neville Goddard says feeling is the secret and it is feeling it as if your dream has come true. What is also important is becoming aware of your mental diet or the chatter that goes on in your mind all day long. It is really important to this process positively.

Anytime you realize you are saying something negative, critical, judgmental or something that is limiting you from living the life you desire, replace that with an affirmation.

Note in your journal any trends that you observe when you are critical of your body. Write down those beliefs. Ask yourself Is this belief serving me? Is this support supporting me attaining my goals and desires? If the answer is no, then it is a limiting belief, and you can override that program with your affirmations.

We think that our circumstances drive our reality. But that is not true. Our beliefs drive our reality, our beliefs about our circumstances drive our reality.

The synchronicities that occur are these random connecting events large and small. They mirror our personal concerns or thoughts. So, what we are focused on, what we are personally concerned with, or what we are personally thinking about, gets mirrored back to us in synchronicities, positive or negative.

The Definite Chief Aim, from Napoleon Hill's *Think and Grow Rich*, along with the Self Confidence formula, are two ways to drive the Bridge of Incidents. It leads you to one thing at a time. It leads you in the direction of your goal.

What your goal is, whatever your desire is, will be received once it is impressed upon the subconscious that you already have what it is that you desire.

Feeling is the secret. There are parallel versions of Earth. Earth is a reflection of your past average state of being /state of consciousness. The bridge, looking back, will show you a series of incidents that your lower mind strings together as the path that it took from point

A to point B. The truth is your state of being is what changes you and the world that you are creating.

Your state of being drives the people, places, and things you are forward to. The path to your desires. They become more reflective of your beliefs, and we are shifting, we are already shifting billions of times per second.

Sometimes with the bridge of incidence if you are looking for a relationship, you want a romantic relationship. Or let us say you want to connect with a certain person.

The bridge is going to lead you to the people, places, and things that you need to interact with, to shift your mindset, your awareness, your consciousness to having the thing that you desire.

More often than not, it is not the person you're going to end up with.

It could be, but more often it is not. It is needed to rendezvous with a specific person. Have your heart broken. Get attached. Learn how to detach, learn how to manage your emotions.

Get ready to have the manifestation that you desire, the relationship that you desire. Sometimes you are not the person you need to be to get what you want. Therefore, the bridge leads you to the people, places and things that will get you ready to have what it is that you desire. So, you cannot be holding on to the way you 'think' you'll receive your desire. You cannot hold onto the relationships(s), jobs, cars, etc. in your current reality. It does not serve you. It actually holds you back. Your human mind "thinks" it knows the way to fulfill your dreams and desires, but your higher mind knows the short cuts. Clinging to the way your human mind "thinks" it'll get there, holds you back.

We are shifting "New Earth." You are never changing the person with which you are dealing. You are only changing your perspective of the person. So, if you are manifesting a SP (Specific Person) or you want to improve a relationship that you have, you are never ever changing the actual person. You are shifting the perspective that you have of the person.

The higher mind conceives, the human mind receives, and the lower mind or the personality perceives.

Our lower mind never generates an idea. It only ever perceives what it is downloading from the universe. It only perceives the result. Translates it. That is why neutrality is key.

Creation is only ever perceived from the highest self. The higher mind equals conception - it conceives.

Buying into a negative belief creates a momentum to a downward spiral negative belief. This triggers negative synchronicities. Negative synchronicities trigger negative circumstances. And it may seem like a string of bad luck. It is unlikely that you will not perceive it as synchronicities. Time and space are the egos perspective on things. Stop insisting it has to unfold a certain way. If you don't insist that means you have no resistance to actual possibilities.

Stop limiting yourself in a negative way. Forcing an SP to be the one when it could come together in an entire package better than you could ever imagine. The higher mind knows better than the ego mind. It knows better than the lower mind.

The quantum field is how to change time. Follow your joy. Your soul knows the easiest and the fastest way through the bridge. When you follow your adventures, your joy and the love that leads you to not need to do all the actions that your human mind thinks that you need to do. Just the ones that light up your soul. Those are the triggers that you are to follow.

Imaginary acts bring you to the feeling of the wish being fulfilled. Let go of being reactive and trying to control the process. This means you don't trust yourself or the process. The reality that you desire already exists but your brain, your ego, your subconscious thinks that it alone knows how to get there. However, your soul knows the path of least resistance. Just manage your state of being. The bridge allows you to change your point of view or your state of being to remember that you already have what you desire.

It is like a mind hack. The outer world actually represents your inner world. You want to raise your awareness, not necessarily your vibration. Your emotions absolutely drive the amount of time, quote unquote, that you take to remember that you already have what you desire.

Being in alignment for one hour can be equal to two weeks' worth of action. The 3D manifestation is you finally remembering that you have what you desire.

There are actions to be taken on the bridge. So, the experience of that action helps shift you to joy, and the shifts will occur faster. Trying implies you do not have what you want. Affirming helps you shift the bridge of incidents. It equals inspired action, and this one step takes you to your delicious dream life.

How are you living? What are you doing here? What are you wearing? How are you feeling? How does it compare to your current reality? The differences are the things you need to change about yourself. The bridge of incidents from Neville Goddard's perspective, is that man desires freedom from his limitation or problem. The first thing man does after he defines his objective is to condition it upon something else. He begins to speculate on the manner of acquiring it. Not knowing that the thing desired has a way of expressing all on its own. He starts planning how he is going to get it there by adding to the Word of God.

The first thing to do is to decide. The second is to plan. If on the other hand he has no plan or conception as to the fulfillment of his desire, then he compromises his desire by modifying it.

He feels if he will be satisfied with less than his basic desire, then he might have a better chance of realizing it. In doing so he takes away from the Word of God, lessens its value.

Individuals and notions alike are constantly violating a natural law. To reach their basic desires they plot and plan. My interpretation is shamefully persisting in knowing your wishes are already fulfilled as God created it to be. Do not "try" to get it. Do not "try to make it less than you desire." Do not "try" to push it down and pretend it has not been created by you for you. It is already perfect for you.

The bridge of incidents helps you let go of the old person that you are and become the new person, the new version of you. If it is a big thing that you are trying to manifest, it will seem as if it takes longer. Expect emotional crashes caused by rejection of your manifestation not appearing as quickly as you would like it.

Number one, process the emotions so that the old timeline can fall away and be careful not to revert back and give up. Persist. Number two, revise, and utilize that to feel any emotions that may come. If anger comes up, release it. Blast it all out to revise.

We are bringing forth heaven on earth. This is Divine Will. I act harmoniously with this on the bridge of incidence.

Thinking of thoughts, we become what we think about. Imagination is one with the universal mind. It not only impresses the subconscious mind, but also the superconscious mind.

Those hunches and inspirations that will come are what you need to create all of the powers within you. Do not form an identity with the bridge. You will go into a lack of perspective trying to force it. Use power only to tell stories that shift you into a positive state. Observe. Do not react to circumstances. Circumstances do not matter. Be propelled forward or be set back and thrown from the bridge of incidents.

Obstacles will begin to be seen as harmonious opportunities. Now they were always harmonious. But we had fears before. It is going to bring us to the harmonious events in order to lead us to the state of the wish fulfilled mind.

The wish fulfilled or reprogrammed the mind in a way that impacts the subconscious of all those in our reality to assist us in the desired state. We are all one release limiting beliefs. These are your steppingstones to create what we want: Infinite Intelligence contributing factors bridge of success. Affirmations shift our confidence which speed up time and causes momentum.

Everything was created with one mind, the Universal Mind and then it is sent out to all the masses. Every atom is seeking to do this projection of the manifestation in the subconscious mind from our

CHAPTER 9

identity or our Higher Mind heaven on earth. We become more harmonious if we cleanse our subconscious mind. We are manifesting the solutions or the keys in the external world to cross the bridge of incidents.

Power is not in the external world. Power is within you, your internal world. Paying attention to the external world is essentially giving away your power. "Trying" to force the outer world to bend to your will. Use personal, internal power instead of force. And lastly, stop taking the shift so seriously you are not even here. There is no you - just having fun.

Enjoy your life one day, one minute, one second at a time. Stop waiting for stuff to come along. Just Be and just be happy. Stop with all the bullshit transformational stuff. You do not need to change anything about you.

The only thing you are changing is the perspective that you have about you. You do this by shifting through millions and millions of parallel realities on offer every second of every day.

What are your desires and what is your ideal future state to be in?

It's like being a time traveler. In fact, you are. Imagine that you are going to a new timeline. Every day that affirms that you are in your new reality. You can feel it from your crown chakra.

Change is like a magnet. It attracts the very things that you are moving toward. Ignore the current timeline that you are on, suspend it in your mind if you can. Think of the new vision of you as traveling, driving, or flying.

As you travel you pass through certain places to get to where you want. If you are driving across the country, you are not going to stop in a state and get out and have a tantrum because your destination (manifestation) has not yet appeared. You are traveling, you are traveling through time, the devil is fear, doubt, and indecision. That is past programming, move beyond that and know that you are creating the new you, moment by moment.

Self-concept and limiting beliefs self-concept are all you need to be aware of to bring about the new desired you and the life you dream of. Our beliefs create feelings that create thoughts. And those thoughts create behaviors. We tend to believe in these behaviors as being us and all that is. But in fact, it's what is underlying the creation of this behavior (from our thoughts and beliefs) that drives your behavior.

Here is something to consider. The 3D world is a mirror.

Now when we usually walk up to a mirror and adjust our clothing, we don't try to change the person in the mirror, we are just adjusting our clothes. When you do that, you do not physically touch the mirror. You do not try to change the outward reflection. You touch your hair or your shirt.

Change yourself and the mirror responds. This is exactly what manifestation is. There is no delay, there is only delay in our mind.

This is the only way that you can change your 3D world. By adjusting yourself, the world corresponds. It's not about what others do, it's about what we do.

Your personality is your personal reality, your self-concept. And your state of being equals your personality or your personal reality.

Your personal reality is how you see yourself in the world. The world that you created. What do you practice feeling? Guilt, shame, anger, frustration, fear? The stronger the emotion the stronger it will impact your physical reality. Thoughts and subsequent emotions create a physical change in your body. A thought or an imaginary act creates the exact same response in your body as an actual event.

Every time you make a decision, you open a new timeline. A parallel reality comes to life and increases the probability that what you decided comes into your 3D reality.

Three things can happen.

Follow through, jump into action. Follow your highest passion. Take the steps as they show up along the bridge of incidents. They are stepping stones that lead you on your new path.

Go back to the old timeline.

Which is a paradigm. The only reason you would go back to the old circumstances or timeline is that you believe that it serves you, serves you better than the new timeline.

Emotions are Energy in motion. These are strategies to get you what you want. What is your strategy? The fuel is going to be positive emotions or negative emotions.

So, emotions are just strategies to get what you want. Let us talk about personality or personal reality. When I am by myself, I have a certain personality. A certain behavior for how I behave and what I do when I am home alone.

I experience my higher self in the easiest and most natural way when I go out into the world. I become or rather - express a different personality.

Depending on the people, places, things that I am in that I am interacting with. I am a different Robin. With each of my children, I am a different version of Robin. I am a different version with my sister. I am a different version of a random stranger. Therefore, I have multiple personalities depending on the people, places, and things with which I am interacting.

Once again this is based on our beliefs and who we believe we are.

Now our self-image self-concept, it is our true identity. We believe that we are a certain way.

So how do you feel about you? What is your identity? Your identity comes from experiences from the time you are born.

In a way you are unlearning some aspects.

As you begin to raise your consciousness you begin to recognize all of the programming blocks, the stories, the negative beliefs, and the circumstances that you adopted.

Those beliefs that gave meaning to your passion, or your new vision brings realization home.

We need to remove the false identity and move it to joy, peace and flow. We want to connect to a vision that reprograms our mind by reprogramming the subconscious into a new and truer identity.

CHAPTER 9

I realize more and more every day who I am by focusing on my vision. My feelings, and emotions are what they reveal about me and my self-concept, I now view myself with the wish fulfilled faith.

Everything always works out for me. Everything I desire comes to me easily and I am the most powerful person on the planet. I am a conscious creator. I am very powerful. I am confident. I am beautiful, I am loved and adored by everyone. I am healthy. I am free. I am safe, I am secure. I am abundant.

There is no self. It is an illusion. We have these mental images of ourselves. How do you feel and see yourself? What do you believe to be true about yourself?

Negative self-concepts and beliefs. These are the blocks.

We create our own reality. We have these false or erroneous beliefs. For example, I ALWAYS SABOTAGE my relationships because I believe all men are narcissistic. Even saying "I always sabotage" is a negative self-fulfilling prophecy. I stopped saying this type of thing.

Remember a thought creates a mental image. The image is created by observations based on past beliefs while gathering evidence to support what you think. Change your thinking, change your world.

You do not really think or create your thoughts. You are receiving thoughts, based on your State of Being. Think of thoughts as currents of energy.

I am both the thinker and the observer of the thoughts I have. And being more aware gives you greater power.

Do you have beliefs and fears that keep coming up for you that you would prefer to let go?

The brain does not know the difference between an imaginary act or an event, an actual event. It accepts whatever you believe to be true. How do we identify our limiting beliefs? First consider an aspect of your life. It could be career finance, wellness, relationships, or your romantic relationship. What do you desire? What is something that you want? That appears to be lacking in your life?

Here is an exercise:

The 5 Whys Technique.

List 5 things that you do not have.

Identify the top five reasons why you do not have these things that you want.

Under each of the 5 write down why you think that you don't have these things?

The next step is then to ask yourself how has believing these (5 limiting answers) been serving you? What benefit do you get?

Name five benefits that you are getting. You may get stuck here. Well, you are supposed to because these are beliefs we have or stories we keep holding on to that are not serving us.

If you answered, "not having (the relationship or new job) protects me and keeps me safe." Or this prevents others from criticizing or laughing at me. Then ask yourself "Who would I be"?

Who would I be if I did not have the fears that held me back?

What would my life be like if I let these fears go? Raising your awareness to these answers is enough for you to let them go consciously.

You can easily let the beliefs go because you recognize they do not serve or support you in the life you desire. They may have served you in the past such as keeping you safe. But the new version of you doesn't need that limited belief.

You can now create affirmations to replace these old beliefs. These are just stories that you have made up in order to protect yourself and keep you safe. Have grace forgive yourself. They did support you in the past. Maybe you went through a really bad breakup or divorce you lost a job, you lost someone close to you. The fact that you are here now means that you are ready, your higher self is guiding you and telling you it is now okay to let go of these stories.

You can now create affirmations to replace these old beliefs.

You can also do a three-minute elevator pitch. It goes like this. Why should someone date you, marry you, hire you or give you money?

Why would someone want to buy your product?

And if you do not know why they should buy your product, then they do not know either.

Your self-concept and your state of consciousness is what drives your new reality.

Step 1: Assume a state of being.

Step 2: A thought follows.

Step 3: Become aware you are not the thinker.

Step 4: Become aware you are the receiver of the thought from the quantum field.

Step 5: The bridge now directs your thoughts and actions, Free Will ends. Then your Higher Self attempts to lead you through the bridge of incidents. The only control you have is the state that you are in.

The bridge of incidents can be described like this. I have my current state of being that I am in right here, right now.

Perhaps I could say in my current state how much money I have in the bank. This is how I could describe reality. I could similarly do this regarding my relationship status, my health, my level of happiness and so on.

These are the ways I view who I am right here right now. But let us say there is a more preferable state that I desire to be in. Let us say I desire to have more money in my bank account, or a new car or move to a new place or live in a newer home.

Whatever that preferred new state is, it exists already. It's available in a parallel reality, in a parallel timeline. This is so because everything has already been created by God. Everything exists here now, there is an infinite number of parallel realities to which we could shift. So, the state that I desire to be in, my ideal preferred state - already exists. The only thing that I need to shift is my state of consciousness, my state of awareness.

They say time flies when you are having fun. So, when you are in the present moment and you are enjoying the present moment, and you are experiencing joy, time seems to speed up. When you are not in the present moment, when you are fearing the future, or obsessing over the past, time slows down. So, the key to entering that bridge of incidents is to be in the present moment. Shift to the state of being that you want to experience.

New positive synchronicities will show up in your world. The joy, right, the people and whatever the new version of you truly seeks.

To Speed up this process follow your joy. Time flies when you are having fun. From your new perspective (from the higher self) the view is different.

From the top of the mountain, you can see the entire valley. You can see the trees, see the roadblocks, and see the shortcuts.

The fun adventures that you could be having you can't see when are on the ground, and not on the mountain top.

Your higher self uses synchronicities, positive or negative to lead you to the direction of your preferred state. Leads you in the direction of the experiences that you need to have to shift your awareness to shift your consciousness, because there already is a version of you that has everything that you desire and is already living in your new preferred state. The only job that you are doing here in this avatar on this planet is shifting your consciousness. Shifting your awareness from the concept that what you desire is removed from you. That there is a thing over there that I want to have. Coming to realize the thing that I desire I already have.

Let us talk about the difference between positive and negative synchronicities. So positive synchronicity is, let us say my current state. I make a few $100,000 a year. My preferred state is that I have a million dollars in the bank account. Well, my focus and my state of being is going to be on what can I do to achieve the million dollars in my bank account?

I am going to be focused on what actions I need to take. I will be focused on a positive direction, and an expansive direction. Willing to take action, willing to take risks. In a state of being where everything is available for me and is happening. I create anew from a state where I feel neutral. A neutral state compared to being in an emotionally reactive state.

I can access the highest state from where I am creating everything.

The synchronicities that occur on my path from my current state to my preferred state because I'm focused on the positive will produce positive synchronicities. They will show up with things in the form of stock tips or an idea to make money or a new way to make money, or a way to make money better than I've been doing before.

Different opportunities, new investments will show up as stepping stones. My financial IQ is going to increase, I will be given opportunities to gain experience and to network with other people who are like minded. These are all samples of positive synchronicities.

My focus is on achieving my goal and everything is happening for me. So I follow my synchronicities. I follow my joy, and I allow that to lead me to the idea or the ideas that will give me my million dollars in the bank.

With negative synchronicity I am in a lower state of consciousness. I am in a victim mentality. Everything happens against me. And if I am in a relationship or I meet someone I will sabotage it because in the past I experienced people cheating on me. Or they left me, or they abused me. Well, because of my state of being, everything happens to me, and I am in lower states of consciousness. I am not in neutrality, or love when I am thinking and feeling about those negative situations. I am perceiving them from lower levels. I am the victim of my reality.

My Synchronicities are going to be providing evidence for my view of relationships being bad, like waking up and seeing my man texting in the middle of the night. My subconscious thoughts and my self-concept take the view that I am the person that gets cheated on, the person that gets abused, the person that does not get a happy, healthy relationship.

My state of being is that I am the victim in my reality. I will continue to receive negative synchronicities, meaning this going to pull me down even further to a non-preferred state. This is a state that I do not want to be in. I do not want to be single. I do not want a relationship to break up. I do not want to be cheated on. And yet, because of my focus and my state of being, that is exactly what happens. I shift to the reality where those things happen to me, instead of shifting to the reality that those things do not happen to me. Once I am aware of this process, I can see that what comes to me in life can be a choice.

ACTIVITY:

1. Identify achievements you've had in the past.

2. Visualize the past achievement and how you felt, the actions you took, the results you had.

3. Can you identify any synchronicities that occurred during this achievement? Oftentimes the series of events that unfold seem as if they were bound to happen, meant to happen, that they would obviously unfold the way they did, but try to identify some of the

gut instincts you had or random occurrences that came out of nowhere.

- Be aware in your current reality that opportunities will arrive, inspiration will be received, magic is happening all around you.

4. Identify from your current goals, some ways you are insisting your goal should appear or unfold.

- Release the insistence that your desire has to be a certain person, place, thing, way.

CHAPTER 10

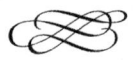

IMAGINATION

"You need imagination in order to imagine a future that doesn't exist." —Azar Nafisi

"Imagination is the beginning of creation. You imagine what you desire, you will do what you imagine and at last you create what you will." —George Bernard Shaw

"Imagination is the eye of the soul." —Joseph Joubert

This is my favorite definition. Imagination is a noun, the faculty or action of forming innovative ideas or images or concepts of external objects not present to the senses.

The ability of the mind to be creative or resourceful is the part of the mind that imagines things. So, the action of forming innovative ideas or images or concepts of external objects do not present to the senses.

We talk about synchronicities, things that are not tangible that I cannot touch, things that are in my mind, the thoughts of my imagination. Now, you can imagine positively, and you can imagine negatively. If you are imagining positive things, you are going to have positive synchronicities. When you are imagining negative things, you are going to have negative synchronicities.

What are you focused on in your imagination? Become aware of the stories that you are telling the images that you are allowing in. What's going on in your mind? As things are happening in your environment how are you reacting to it? Not just at a physiological level but how is your mind reacting to it? Are you thinking oh, this is the same failure over and over again?

Are you imagining, and saying to yourself, "I am going to be successful"?

Are you creating positive affirmations? This is going to happen for me. It is going to happen; I am never going to give up. It must happen. I insist that it is going to happen in my reality. Because I am confident. I am going to keep going. I trust myself. I trust the process. I trust my creation.

Now a lot of people tell me that they cannot imagine. They have trouble visualizing and that isn't true. They are just not aware of the visual images that are going on within their mind.

I would have said the same thing several years ago, until I started to meditate, and I started to practice focusing on what was going through my mind. Meditation is not to quiet the mind. Meditation is to tune in to what you want to focus on. The tune into a specific thing one thing at a time. Meditation teaches you how to focus.

You want to learn how to turn your life around? Then learn how to meditate. Learn how to be a conscious observer of your thoughts of your imagination. Because when you do that, you can stop the negative past from opening the negative story. You can redirect the negative synchronicities, imagine the preferred state, a more preferred timeline with positive outcomes, positive synchronicities.

Throughout my career I have observed many people make a very pivotal decision. Moving from being in a victim mentality to imagining their preferred state.

For example, they may have got a benefit from being addicted to the victim mentality.

Thinking that by being the best victim on the planet, it gave them some type of status.

Imagine thinking that if I am a big, huge victim that it elevated me in some type of way. This was what I experienced myself. I was stuck in a victim mentality. It was not until I made a commitment to myself that I was going to take responsibility for my life, that I realized that I had to give up being the victim in my story. I had to give up being the victim in my reality. I had to stop just giving up and saying Yep, that is it. I am a victim.

You see, that is why I stopped trusting myself. That is why my confidence was lacking. Because I kept giving up on myself. I kept repeating the same story over and over. I would say I am a victim and throw my hands up. It is the government's fault. It is my parents' fault. It is my family's fault. It is my ex-husband's fault. It is everyone else's fault in the world except for mine.

When you claim no responsibility, this is what eats away at your trust. That is what kills your confidence. Many people are addicted to the victim mentality. It is everyone else's fault. Why I am not successful. I am a woman. I am this... I am that... listing out all the reasons why I cannot be successful. Those are lies. Those that are choosing to stay in the victim mentality. Those are lower states of consciousness. Everything is happening against me.

We are shifting into higher states, raising our state of consciousness. We are taking accountability. We are taking responsibility. We are learning to trust ourselves. We are going to build our confidence. We are not going to give up. We are not going to throw our hands up and say it is the system. We are going to find a unique way. We are going to get creative. We are going to use our imagination to solve these problems and focus on the solutions instead of the problems. I am going to focus on collaborating and building and solving instead of affirming that I am a victim.

In my reality, all day, every day I am creating.

So, imagine what is happening throughout the day? Are you even aware of what you are imagining? What images are floating through your head? Because those things are what is creating your reality. Those things are further affirming your reality. Providing affirmation to stay in that current state. Until you become aware of what it is that you are imagining, through your thoughts through your feelings through your reactions you cannot change your focus.

In the study of psychology, imagination generally refers to the ability to mentally represent sensations that are not physically present. So, for example if a person is thinking about a lemon, whether they are tasting it or smelling it, they can imagine in their mind how a lemon taste.

The neocortex and thalamus are responsible for controlling the brain's imagination along with many of the brain's other functions such as consciousness and abstract thought.

So, if our subconscious is creating our reality, 95% of what is created is from our subconscious.

It is being created by these thoughts, these ideas, the things that we are imagining in our brain.

If you are focused on the past, you will keep creating what you have always created.

If you are focused on the future and there's fear, if you are imagining that things are not going to go well then that is a reason to procrastinate.

It can be why we sabotage because we are afraid of what is being created in the future. But if you are in the present moment, if you stay in the present moment, and decide that no matter what you will have a successful outcome. No matter what happens, you just stay focused.

Circumstances in 3D do not matter.

Staying focused in the present moment I manage my state of being. I am going to manage my focus and my thoughts.

And what I am imagining is seeing those thoughts, creating those mental images in our brain.

The mental images stir up a feeling, so the image paired with the feeling is what creates the future.

There are frequency and intensity of frequency. Not in terms of radio frequencies, but the frequency of our creative imagination. The frequency of thought, of the imagining and the intensity of the feeling is what you are creating next in your environment. This gives out a frequency, a certain vibration.

So, if you are wondering why something just blew up in your life, you may have to go back and retrace your steps. What were you thinking about? How often were you thinking about it? What was the intensity?

What was going on in your imagination?

What was the intensity of the feeling that you were feeling?

So, frequency multiplied by intensity equals future reality.

Knowing this I am going to make sure that I stay in the present moment. And I am going to manage my focus and I am going to manage the mental images that come into play. And if by chance, they go down a negative path, I am going to quickly pull myself off that path and put myself back on the path that I want to be on.

I am committed to managing what I am going to focus on and my success.

Find out what it is that you want. What is the outcome? What is your intention? What are you setting out to do? What are you intending to do?

What is the outcome you desire?

What is the next step? What opportunities do I already have in front of me, what opportunities are in front of me of which I am not even aware?

I want to take advantage of all those opportunities. Who are the people that I could reach out to? Who can help me achieve what it is that I desire?

It is so easy to change. We can change in an instant. It is called a paradigm shift.

I underwent hypnosis and I quit smoking immediately. Immediately, I had a complete shift in my beliefs.

If you could detach your beliefs from your reality and look like a detached observer, it will be easy for you to identify the limiting beliefs. And subsequently accept a new belief or change.

How you do one thing is how you do everything.

Always focus on the outcome that you desire.

Our brain does these three things, specifically our RAS.

1. We like to generalize information.

2. We delete information.

3. We distort information.

In learning beliefs, we have a belief that there is a benefit to us holding on to that limiting belief. There is some benefit to believing what we are believing, or we would not believe it.

It may be that I am going to make a fool out of myself, so I won't take the risk. If I make more money I am going to have more responsibilities or there will be more risk or if I put myself out there. I am going to get hurt or people will steal from me if I make more money. There is some type of underlying belief.

Now these beliefs are formed to protect us so you cannot get upset, angry, ashamed. Whatever you believe, you are going to constantly find evidence to support that.

To stop procrastinating people say they want to be more disciplined. They want to get more things done. They say they do not want to be lazy. However, you will follow through on 99.9% of the things that you have ever committed to do.

You do not procrastinate on the majority of the things that you set out to do. You are just not hyper focused, aware of those things. You are only hyper super focused, aware of the things that you are not getting done. And you got to look at those things that you are not getting done. Is there a belief there? There is some underlying belief that is protecting you to procrastinate.

For me, I used to put off paying the bills. It was at a time when I had a lot of issues financially. I was heavily in debt. I had $30,000 in medical bills. I could barely make ends meet. I dreaded and put off paying my bills every single month to the point where things would get shut off. I was procrastinating not because I did not want to pay my bills, not because I was lazy. Not because I was not disciplined for any of those reasons, except that when I sat down to do the bills, I would be sick and I would be stressed. I would be upset. I did not know how I was going to pay everything.

I knew some things would have to fall between the cracks and I did not want to make those decisions. Those were really hard decisions. Do I pay for food? Or do I pay for gas? Do I pay the dentist, or do I pay the electric? Those important needs were not getting met and yes, I was procrastinating putting it off. This was because I had my thinking aimed to protect me from facing a stressful situation. It is always going to protect us. I did not want to deal with reality. So yes, I was avoiding sitting down and facing the reality that I only had a couple of hundred dollars and yet my bills were thousands of dollars.

Every behavior that we have is taking us towards pleasure or away from pain so if you are procrastinating or sabotaging this is why.

You are moving towards pleasure and away from pain. What I know gives me pleasure. What I do not know (artificially) relieves my pain. So I avoid facing the finances.

Sitting down and physically paying my bills, I did not know what I was going to find. I did not know what the totals were. I did not know what was in my bank account. I did not know what I was going to be able to pay, or not pay.

I was avoiding pain, the unknown. The crazy thing about it is those bills all got paid somehow. Someway those bills all got paid. I was procrastinating, avoiding pain, or thinking I was avoiding pain and really, I was not. Fear of the unknown is what we are often trying to move away from.

What we do not know is what we fear moving towards something that is new. So, changing something up. There's fear in the unknown. We think it is scary to do that.

I do not know if it is going to be painful. I do not know if it is going to be pleasurable.

Why do people avoid relationships? They are moving towards pleasure away from pain. They do not want to get their heart broken.

If I fear the unknown, then the unknown is what I fear.

If I fear something, I am just going to avoid it. We love what we want, and we fear what we do not want.

There are two motivators:

1. Pain

2. Pleasure

Pain is the unknown. I could possibly have pain. When we are sabotaging or procrastinating, we can set an anchor. We can set some type of anchor, like squeezing our hand together and putting our nails into the palm of our hand.

Instead, recall some sort of mantra or belief system. A positive reminder that you got this.

You perceive that there is some type of fear.

In addition to this, every emotion is a strategy. It is some type of strategy to get your needs met. They act as anchors to elicit a certain state of being to immediately pull you out of the negative or the fear-based state and move quickly back into a higher state.

There's always intention behind emotions, or some type of strategy or intent behind every emotion.

You want to align your values to the outcome that you desire. You have got to become the master of your emotions.

The way to master your mind; you master your thoughts and emotions is by focus. You master your focus, whatever you focus on is what you are going to get. Are you focused on your success or on your failure?

It is just a choice. It is a choice. What do you choose? Sometimes we are not even aware of what we are focusing on. We are focused on things that make us upset.

You tend to keep pulling yourself back. Am I going to succeed, or I am going to fail? You pull back due to fear of failure.

Focus on the goal. Ignore the circumstances, routine plus consistency equals outcome. I will say this again. Routine plus consistency equals outcome. You got yourself to a state where the solution is going to present itself. Shift from the state of being where you created the problem. Shift to the state where you are moving towards the solution.

You have to shift your state of being. Focus on the idea that this problem is already solved. It is already solved. Time does not even exist. Everything exists as one so this problem that has been created in my mind is already solved.

Keep moving forward. Because it is going to resolve itself.

Become aware of your unconscious desires. A lot of people fall into a category where they have desires, but they push them away. I meet a lot of people especially in the spiritual community who say I do not want money; it is the root of all evil. Money is bad. I do not want to change. I do not want to make money. It is not good. There is so much corruption. There is this... there is that, but deep down inside they desire money.

They desire comfort, they desire abundance. They desire to travel; they desire to take care of their needs. They desire to not worry about money. And yet here they are spouting off to the world because they believe that is what society wants them to do. Because society has told them money is the root of all evil.

Money is bad. Bad people have money. Everything should be free. That is what their parents taught them or their neighbor or their self-righteous boyfriend or spouse imparted to them. So they deny their desires and yet they wonder why they are miserable.

You need to be honest with yourself. I am very honest with my desires, I love money, I love the freedom that money and abundance provides for me. I want all the money that I can make. I want to take my kids on adventures so I can spend more time with my family.

So, I can create good memories. I love nice things. I love having a nice car. I love living in a nice home. I love eating tasty food. I love traveling. I love staying in really nice places.

I refuse to deny my desires. Many people refuse their desires. They are cheating themselves and that is why they are miserable. You have to make those unconscious desires conscious.

What are your values? Align your higher values and behaviors. At times we procrastinate and sabotage when we think that the new activity is going to take away from our values. That they are threatening those values. You want to incorporate all those values and things into one vision. So they are not threatening you. They are not competing with each other. You have to imagine that all your values are being met no matter what happens.

Stay focused. You focus on physiology and self-talk. Imagine that it is already done. Imagine that all those values are met.

So that the focus, the physiologic physiology and the self-talk align. A definite chief aim finds the contradictions in your values. Find the ones that are competing.

Hypnosis attacks the identity. It instantly changes the identity therefore changes the behaviors that we are addicted to. The habit placebos work. Visualize what the most confident person, the avatar of me looks like. Visualize the version of me that has everything that I desire.

The version of me that is confident that I will always succeed no matter what. You have to influence yourself. Prime yourself for your day. Set the intention of how you want to feel and keep bringing your focus back to that feeling. It takes practice. You need to build the habit, but you want to prime yourself for success and excellence.

The raising of your awareness is going to pick that up. If you are thinking negative thoughts, you are priming yourself to lose. If you are thinking positive thoughts, you are priming yourself to win and take action. Priming removes the fear that blinds you. My values are always going to get me what I want.

We have subconscious and conscious values. Truly confident people make others feel confident. Fake confidence makes others feel small.

Confidence is contagious.

Insecurity is contagious.

You should be asking yourself every day, does my behavior match my intention?

Am I constantly behaving and taking action in my chosen direction?

Decide every day what your intentions are going to be and what are you trying to get out of the day. Intention has to match behavior. For you to have a change of behavior you have to have a change in intention and it's automatic, it's habitual.

What you focus on is what is going to create your emotions.

I.e., motion, energy in motion, action equal results, focus equals emotions, equals motion, equals action.

What percentage of your day are you focused on what you want?

ACTIVITY:

1. Your Personality is your Personal Reality. Identify your top 20 personality traits.

2. Now identify the top 20 personality traits of the people who have the life or things you desire. Use your imagination.

3. Become aware of the differences between the two. Identify the personality traits you will need to adopt in order to become the person you desire to be.

4. Imagine being that person.

CHAPTER 11

FOCUS AND PRIMING

"If you can dream it, you can do it." –Walt Disney

"A person is what he or she thinks about all day long." –Ralph Waldo Emerson

"Everything you want is out there waiting for you to ask. Everything you want also wants you. But you have to take action to get it." –Jack Canfield

I learned this activity from Chase Hughes, at a Mindset event I attended last year in Los Angeles. He is Behavioral Analyst, Former Military, Former CIA Agent.

There is an app you can download that ages your face. You upload a current picture and it creates what you will look like in the future.

Age your face and post it all over your house. Save it as your lock screen on your phone. Use it as a Quantum jumping tool. Feel the future version of you. Let it motivate, guide, and lead you in the direction you want to go in.

Keep thinking about that future self. How do you want that future self to feel about you today? Use that person to guide you to motivate you to keep you going to keep you focused. What would your future self-want you to be doing? Are you fulfilling the needs of your future self?

It will be great to look back at the past version of you with gratitude. So build that relationship with your future, your future self. It is going to help you focus and develop discipline, you will be able to influence yourself.

Focus on your journey, not your destination. This forces your attention to where you want it to go. Fear increases our perception that the likelihood of a negative circumstance is going to occur. Probability increases in our mind.

Fear makes us more predictable, delayed gratification equals discipline when you place your future self needs ahead of your own present one. This is important, discipline equals delayed gratification when you place your future self needs ahead of your own present one.

Depression is unmet expectations, unmet values, unmet needs. The reward of the future is more important than the reward of the present. Prioritize the needs of your future self or the desire of the present self. The one you select should be focused on your future self-act from that future you perspective.

Most failures we can attribute to us from the present self-neglect discipline, present tense self prioritizes the wellbeing of the future self. We have three selves. The first is the past self, second is the present, and the third is the future. Habit versus discipline. Discipline is only needed in the first week. In the first seven days you need discipline. After that it becomes a habit. Fear is focus. E is for emotional investment. A is for agitation. R is for repetition. You have to brainwash yourself with what you focus on. Picture your future self. Imagine it as vividly as you can.

Choose the ingredients that you want. See yourself eating well, exercising, wearing the clothes you want to wear, going to the gym. Or whatever it is that you wish for in your future.

Who are you hanging out with?

Imagining as much as you can about the preferred future is all you need to do. Those are the ingredients that give you permission to act a certain way and to be a certain thing that you desire to be.

Be responsible for what you see and feel, take responsibility and know you create your future.

Give yourself permission, automatically assuming that you are listened to and that you are the leader. Get comfortable with your end goal. Imagine yourself successful in that time period - in the future. Create a slideshow in your mind. Create an avatar of the person who has everything that they desire.

Imagine yourself standing up giving a TED Talk, as an activity of your own success.

Successful people prioritize time over money and sell time for money. Stop valuing money, ask yourself how I get the most out of this with the least amount of time. This produces immediate action. It helps you to stop procrastinating.

What is the most I can do in one hour? What is the most that I can get out of one hour? Every action makes waves. Imagine taking ten actions and it will make big waves. You could focus on making fifty big actions a month.

Addictive behaviors like drinking, smoking, marijuana, food, sex, porn, waiting to the last-minute and sabotaging are from a lack. These are all behaviors where we are avoiding something else. Many of us are avoiding feeling, we are pushing it down, we are pushing those feelings down.

We want to mask that uncomfortable noise. So we do something else to release that energy. In meditation, it is a safe space in our minds where we can do this more positively. We are usually looking for validation, love, acceptance and worth.

You are only ever focused on two things: what is wanted or unwanted, identify what is unwanted and start focusing on it. Limiting beliefs come from fear our RAS generalizes, deletes, and distorts. So, money is bad. This Is a generalized statement. It deletes every other situation where it worked, where it was not bad, where it saved us, where it fed us. And then it distorts this, maybe I didn't work as hard. Maybe I don't deserve it. Find out all the areas that you have generalized, deleted, and distorted information.

A state of being is a strategy. All emotions are strategies.

We want to condition the RAS to get rid of limiting beliefs. That is through positive and negative emotions. Again, emotions are strategies. If I am sad, RAS is going to pick everything to match our state, it is always taking us towards that goal or that intention. Whatever our state is, it is taking us further towards that continued state.

Emotions are feedback telling me if I am making progress towards the things that I want or not making progress towards the things I want. If I am focused on what I want, I am headed in the right direction. If I am focused on what I do not want, then I am going the opposite direction.

When you aren't in the preferred state, identify your goal. Control your state of being as this increases the speed and the intensity. our RAS will strategize emotions and create the strategy.

Consistency equals outcome.

Scarcity mindset isn't just about money and abundance. Scarcity/Abundance can refer to time, resources, attention, etc.

You want to take effective, inspired action. Checking off tasks on the list means nothing. You want to consider what is going to give you the highest return on investment (ROI).

Are you in the right mindset? What is your state of being? What are you focused on? Are you focused on your success? Are you confident in your success? Take effective action. Use the highest leverage action that you can take. Learn high leverage skills. Maximize your cash flow and minimize time wasting activities. Leverage asking questions, know when you need to write down all your details, everything you do produces results.

Confidence is the number one thing to transform your life. Everything falls into place. Your dating life, business, and life in general.

Do you want to be more confident? Well, what do you want to be more confident about? Confidence is only one of two things. I am confident that I am going to succeed, or I am confident that I am not.

In the past I have not taken action because I was confident I was going to fail.

What is the difference between a successful and a non-successful person? It's the mindset. Success is defined differently by all of us.

Five years ago, I never imagined I would be where I am today. Successful, healthy, and finally, happy. I was very confident I was going to fail.

Today, I am confident and I am always successful. Confident that everything always works out in my favor.

Mindset is the most important thing.

Be confident you are going to be successful or be confident you are going to fail.

It's important to be aware of how you react or respond to the things that happen in your life. How we view the circumstances of our life or our natural state of being is important.

You want to break the gap between today and where you want to be. Let go of the now to receive the new. Have Confidence in the person who has done it a million times.

Focus on your outcome, your goals, clarity of outcome.

Where are you going? Be clear about it. Have 100% extreme focus only on what you want, stop focusing on negative outcomes. What you focus on is what you get. Take action that produces results. Your focus creates the discipline to focus on the outcome that is your GPS.

Bring your power back into your body and learn how to receive.

If you are not aware of this - it is called a pattern interrupt.

Does habit drive your behavior? Maybe you have a tough time getting out of bed every morning and you hit the snooze button. And let us say you want to get out, you want to get up early. You want to go to the gym. When you first get the thought that you are too tired to get up this makes it harder to take the action to live your dreams. But you let fear get in the way the split second the thought about the thing pops in. This neural hack helps.

Count backwards - 5, 4, 3, 2, 1. This takes five seconds for the brain to search through the evidence of why you should or should not do something. Before it does, you need to interrupt. This confuses the brain. It stops the train in its tracks and has to create a new neural pathway in the brain. (from Mel Robbins book '5 Second Rule). In this way the old pathway, the computer wire that led to the negative evidence just got derailed. The next thing to do is just to take action.

Taking action not only gives you the result that you intended to do, but it also creates a new neural pathway. It is creating new evidence to support the reasons why you should do the thing which will then override the old evidence. This occurs the entire time your brain chemistry is changing. As your focus is changing, so is your life.

Another way to reprogram your mind is to practice gratitude. When RAS, the filter on your brain, seeks out evidence to support you, then by practicing gratitude, your brain will go on a search and seize mission to find more things to be grateful about. Not only are you going to start appreciating more and more the blessings that you have, but you are going to start seeing the number of blessings that you did not notice before. You are going to start seeing new opportunities coming your way to be more grateful for and your RAS is now super hyper aware of the environment and starts to notice more information. It is going to lead you to be more grateful.

What you focus on grows.

They did this study, they found on average that we unlock our phone over one hundred times a day. You unconsciously are looking at your lock screen at least one hundred times a day. What is on your lock screen on your phone? You can use this habit of looking at your phone to send messages to your subconscious. What is on your lock screen? Make an image with words relating to your top five goals for the week, the month, or the year. And make it your lock screen. You will be subconsciously reminded approximately one hundred times a day of what to FOCUS on. Your RAS will be reminded to be on the lookout for the things that will bring you the things on your list, the opportunities, the places, the people, the synchronicities.

Make a vision board. Print out pictures of all the things that you desire. Put them up on your bathroom mirror. Type up your chief aim and your self-confidence formula. Make a voice recording of those, play them in the morning and before you go to bed. Record your affirmations. Play those as soon as you wake up in the morning and right before you go to bed.

ACTIVITY:

1. Make a picture, aging you into the future. Imagine being that future person. What are they doing? Where are they living? What dreams have they made come true? What advice would they give you today?

2. Write down your top 5 goals for the next 12 months. Take a picture of them. Make them the lock screen on your phone as a reminder several hundred times a day. What you focus on, grows.

3. Make a vision board of all your desires. Post them in your bathroom, bedroom, office, car, refrigerator as a constant reminder of the direction you are moving in.

4. Imagine giving a Ted Talk. What would you say about yourself? About yourself? How you achieved success?

CHAPTER 12

AUTO SUGGESTION AND HYPNOSIS

"What you think you become. What you feel you attract. What you imagine you create." —Buddha

"Beware of what you set your heart upon...for it shall surely be yours." —Ralph Waldo Emerson

"To bring anything into your life, imagine that it's already there." —Richard Bach

---

Auto suggestion is influencing one's own attitudes, behavior, or physical condition by mental processes other than conscious thought as often used in self-hypnosis. At the beginning of the 20th century the apothecary Emile Coue developed a psychological technique related to the placebo effect. It is a form of self-induced suggestion in which individuals guide their own thoughts, feelings, or behaviors. Whenever you catch yourself in a negative self-talk or anything where you are expressing fear and doubt or self-loathing, you stop. And then delete it or erase it.

I use a technique where I destroy and uncreate one thought and then replace it with a more empowering belief or thought.

It is a way of describing your own thoughts, feelings, and beliefs to influence your behaviors and actions.

This is key. The behaviors and the actions that are taken from the thoughts and beliefs that you have. This is what is creating your physical 3D reality.

We live in a physical 3D reality and physical action creates your reality. So, if you have a belief or a thought that is limiting you, it is also limiting the behavior that you are going to take, and it is also limiting the reality that you are creating for yourself.

The most important part of the journey process, the most crucial point is the effect of limiting beliefs.

When you hold limiting beliefs, such as I am not strong, I am not lovable, there are no good men out there, those types of beliefs inform your behavior and the actions that you are going to take in 3D reality.

So, if I am not strong, I am never going to do anything requiring physical or mental strength. I am going to shy away from it. Why would I have a belief that I am not strong? Why would I do something to prove to myself that I am not strong? I already have the belief. I do not need to reinforce it. So therefore, I am not going to do anything that is going to require physical or mental strength. I am not going to take risks. I am not going to go on adventures. I will be living in fear of being hurt.

If I am not lovable. I am not going to put myself in situations where people can either love me or reject me. Why would I take the risk of getting rejected? Remember, our subconscious believes that it is death, that rejection is death. So why would I take risks and put myself in positions where I could potentially get rejected when rejected means death in my brain.

In order to protect myself I closed the road leading me to rejection. But by closing that road, I also closed the door leading me to love. So if I have a belief that there are no good guys, there are no good men my RAS is going to go out and find evidence to support this. Okay, so my brain, its job is to seek out evidence to support whatever my belief is. It does this whether the belief is positive or negative, the RAS simply supports the belief.

My old belief was that all men are going to treat me badly. The RAS is going to be filtering everything in my awareness to only bring the evidence that men are bad.

So then I won't go out on a date. Even if I do go out on a date, every man that I spend time with, I will already have the assumption that he is no good. And my thoughts and behaviors will be ahead of me, down the road already having "decided" that this is not a good guy. I am not going to take the right behaviors, the right actions towards this person, I am not going to treat them well. I have already made an assumption that they are not a good guy. So, make sure to give them a chance to know at the first sign that they are "bad". I am going to be running away and it creates a self-fulfilling prophecy that there are no good guys out there.

Let's examine the placebo effect. Which is a suggestion to the mind that something will fix or cure it. When one is given a placebo or a sugar pill, a beneficial effect is produced by the placebo drug versus actual treatment. So treatment which cannot be attributed to the properties of the placebo itself must be due to the patient's belief in the treatment to the placebo. The whole thing about the placebo is the belief by the person instead of taking the placebo (the fake drug or fake treatment). They believe they are going to be healed.

Dr. Hew Len is a physician in Hawaii who worked at a mental institution. It is reported that he healed 1000's of patients in the years that he worked there, but he had never seen or treated any one of them. He would just read the patient's chart and imagine them becoming healthy and over time they did become healthy. Jesus had that same power; he imagined the person healthy. Any person that came to him that was sick was healed. He would just imagine them healed. And because the person coming to him had a belief that he had the power to heal them that was also their belief. So here you have your co-creating. Both parties are believing in the power of the miracle, and they would actually be cured.

Interestingly, when Jesus was in his hometown in Jerusalem, his power was diminished. His healing powers were diminished in Jerusalem, which is the hometown where he grew up. There are people that knew him in his hometown and because they knew him before he became known as a big healer, they just looked at him like he was a normal guy. The majority of his town folk did not see him as being a powerful healer. Therefore, his powers were diminished when he was working with those people. This was because of their belief; they did not have the belief that he could heal them. They lacked the belief that he had any type of superpowers.

Many years ago when I was diagnosed with cancer, I researched all different types of treatment on cancer. One of the interesting facts that I found out about when people are diagnosed with cancer is that their tumor tends to grow or get worse immediately after initial diagnosis. It is because immediately when you get that diagnosis, you have so much fear going through your body and through your brain. The thoughts are all fear-based thoughts. I am going to die; I am going to lose my hair from chemo treatment. It is going to get worse. It is going to spread; it is going to kill me. This fear just literally takes over and creates a reality where that disease becomes worse. Once you start getting treatment the size of the tumor starts to go down, decrease, and you get better. This is what happened to me.

However, I went to work on my thoughts. I negated what I was creating with my beliefs and my thoughts. Instead of my tumor getting bigger from my fear-based thoughts I negated this by intercepting those thoughts.

I have also read the studies of people with multiple personalities. Each personality has a different health issue or health condition. There was a person with three distinctly different personalities. One personality would need glasses and the other two did not need glasses. The second personality was an insulin dependent diabetic. The other two personalities were not insulin dependent. And then let us say that the third had no health issues. The physical health issues were dependent on the personality that was in charge. Their reality changed as instantly as their personality changed.

Each personality has a different state of being, thoughts, beliefs, and definitions. Therefore, the physical manifestations are different with each personality. Let us talk about personality. Personality can be equated to a particular state of being, your personality is your personal reality, how we feel about or perceive the world. This is my personal reality. This is what I am experiencing here in 3D.

So, my state of being, my thoughts, my beliefs, my definitions make up my personal reality. My personality, formed over time by my beliefs, is how I develop a specific personality.

We tend to say "Oh, that is just how that person is." Have you ever known an aunt or an uncle who are cranky all the time? Oh, that is just their personality.

In Tarot reading and astrology, certain aspects of each of the signs, i.e., sun sign moon sign, and all the different placements. There are certain personality traits that the signs assume.

I always ask the question: "What came first? The chicken or the egg"? Did I develop the personality or was I born with this personality? Did the date and time that I came into this world - and the planetary placements really shape my personality? Or was it the social influences? I consider that my personal reality is a little bit of both. I think I could argue both sides to that equation.

There are mind hacks to counteract limiting beliefs or influences on you. Auto suggestion is one way to counteract or treat the limiting beliefs or the symptoms.

We can use affirmation. Affirmations are "I am" statements that are more powerful, more empowering than the original belief. The aim is to counter the limiting belief that I am successful, I am confident I am healthy. I am sexy.

Ask formations is another way. These are really fantastic ways to play with your mind and your subconscious. I like to have fun with this stuff. Ask yourself questions about the reality that you want to create. Give yourself a problem and your RAS will run out there and try to solve it for you.

This is how it works. So, you are going to ask questions. Let us say for instance, in my preferred reality I want to be a millionaire. Instead of saying affirmations, I am a millionaire. I am wealthy beyond measure, bla bla bla. I could ask things like what am I going to do with all this money? Now that I make millions of dollars, what am I going to do with all this money? Where am I going to invest all this money? I have thousands of dollars coming in. Where am I going to travel, what adventures shall I take? I need to work on my financial IQ so that I know how I'm going to invest all this money. I need to work on my financial IQ. Where can I work on my financial IQ? The aim is to ask certain questions as if you already have what the desired reality is and now you need to solve the new problems presented from this new reality. This triggers your brain to go out on a search and seizure mission to find the answers. You will get those positive or negative synchronicities along the way. You are going to uncover other ways to make money. You are going to find ways that lead in the direction of more money and will give you more opportunities.

Take action.

Ask formations can be highly enjoyable. Ask questions like how did I get so lucky? How did I end up with such an amazing man?

Maybe I want to get married, but I do not have a man in my life. The ask formations will consist of me thinking of problems that I would have. That is, problems I would have assuming that that desire has already been filled.

So, I ask myself. Where are we going to get married?

What venue are we going to get married at? What kind of dress am I going to wear? When are we going to have this wedding? What kind of food are we going to serve? Where are we going to have our honeymoon?

It puts you in a state of being. It puts you in a state consciousness, acting as if your desire has already been fulfilled. Subsequently your brain must go on a search and seizure mission. Let us say a tunnel exists or a new timeline exists now where you are getting married.

Persisting in that line of thinking, the universe must conform. It must conform because it has to deliver to you someone that you are going to marry.

You can also use hypnosis, and this is getting a deep state such as the theta state and replacing or reprogramming those thoughts that you have originally with the preferred new way.

This is a cool example. Let me tell you a story. Hypnosis is extremely powerful. I have been using this for a couple of years. I create self-hypnosis that I use. I also utilize other hypnosis, such as guided hypnosis videos. I use these in order to reprogram my own mind. Last year, I wanted to quit smoking. I have beliefs that smoking is bad for you. Okay, now the opposite of that can be true. If I have a strong belief that smoking is not bad for me, smoking is not going to kill me, smoking is not going to do any damage to my body. That is true. Your beliefs create your reality. I have such a strong belief though, that smoking is not good for me. Therefore, I knew I needed to get rid of smoking. So, I had a session with one of my coaches, who is an amazing hypnotist. He hypnotized me. He associated smoking with having a cigarette in my hand, inhaling cigarettes, smoking, the act of smoking, the thought of smoking with a disgusting raw chicken that had been laying in a dumpster for weeks, moldy and with flies all over it.

I quit smoking immediately. To this day, I have not gone back. I cannot even be around people smoking. I cannot even think about it. I am getting nauseous just thinking about it. That is how strong he made that replacement association.

So, the association now that I have to smoke is not pleasure. It is not relaxing.

ACTIVITY:

There are 5 main aspects in our life:

1. Career

2. Finance

3. Health and Wellness

4. Relationships

5. Romantic Relationships

1. For each aspect, identify all the limiting or negative beliefs you have about it.

2. For each aspect, identify all the limiting or negative beliefs the aspect has about you.

3. Write out a comprehensive list of all the limiting or negative beliefs

4. Alongside each of the limiting beliefs, re-write them as positive affirmations.

5. Record these and loop them - play them every morning when you get up and every night before you go to bed.

6. As these are impressed on your subconscious, you'll want to repeat the exercise, as you may find new limiting beliefs. Each time I reach a certain threshold, and can't break through it, I do this exercise.

CHAPTER 13

SUMMARY OF ACTIVITIES

ACTIVITY:

1. Identify 10 beliefs you had as a child that you learned were untrue as an adult.

2. Identify your thoughts on the reason(s) you were taught those beliefs. Don't be judgmental on this. Try to identify the root of the reasoning. In most cases it's out of fear. But Fear of what?

3. Give yourself permission to explore more ideas and beliefs that you've learned in your life, that may not be true or real.

ACTIVITY:

1. Identify some beliefs you currently have about yourself that are 'negative'.

2. List the evidence you have gathered throughout your life that supports this belief.

3. What would you change about this belief - if you could?

ACTIVITY:

1. Identify the TOP 5 emotions you feel on a daily basis.

2. Identify the % of time you are in that state.

3. Where do you fit on the Scale? Is it possible to imagine that your reality is based on your State of Being? That your circumstances are driven by the feelings you have on a daily basis?

4. Identify how you would prefer to feel every day.

ACTIVITY:

For each of the Needs, identify how you are currently getting these met and then identify new ways you can have them met.

Hierarchy of Needs	Definition	How you currently meet these:	New ways for you to meet these needs:
Physiological Needs	Basic human needs such as water, food, shelter, comfort, etc.		
Safety Needs	The desire for security, stability, and safety		
Social Needs	The desire for affiliation including friendship and belonging		
Esteem Needs	The desire for self-respect, and respect from others		
Self-Actualization	The desire for self-fulfillment		

ACTIVITY:

1. Identify the top needs you get met consistently.

2. Identify the top needs you want to get met consistently.

3. What strategy have you used in the past to get your needs met?

4. Is there anything you would change about those strategies?

ACTIVITY:

1. Identify your top values.

2. Identify ways/strategies you currently meet/attempt to meet them.

3. Identify ways they may be competing against each other.

4. Create a slide or a little movie in your head where all your needs and values are being met simultaneously. As you begin to work with this image, see the resistance slip away.

ACTIVITY:

1. Identify your current beliefs about an aspect of your life. Pick one aspect below.

- Career
- Finance
- Health/Wellness
- Relationships
- Romantic Relationships

Brainstorm every belief you have about that subject/aspect.

2. Identify the negative or limiting beliefs.

3. Identify the beliefs that aspect has towards you. For instance, if this is for your career, identify all the reasons your employer won't promote you, or pays you little money. Identify what you BELIEVE is the reason you don't have what you want.

4. Take all of the negative beliefs and write out positive affirmations to counter these beliefs.

ACTIVITY:

1. Identify the top 3-5 goals you want to achieve.

2. Write/Type your Self-confidence formula.

3. Post your goals and Self-Confidence formula all over your home and office.

4. Read it daily.

5. I record mine along with my affirmations and play it several times throughout the day.

ACTIVITY:

1. Identify achievements you've had in the past.

2. Visualize the past achievement and how you felt, the actions you took, the results you had.

3. Can you identify any synchronicities that occurred during this achievement? Oftentimes the series of events that unfold seem as if they were bound to happen, meant to happen, that they would obviously unfold the way they did, but try to identify some of the gut instincts you had or random occurrences that came out of nowhere.

Be aware in your current reality that opportunities will arrive, inspiration will be received, magic is happening all around you.

4. Identify from your current goals, some ways you are insisting your goal should appear or unfold.

Release the insistence that your desire has to be a certain person, place, thing, way.

ACTIVITY:

1. Your Personality is your Personal Reality. Identify your top 20 personality traits.

2. Now identify the top 20 personality traits of the people who have the life or things you desire. Use your imagination.

3. Become aware of the differences between the two. Identify the personality traits you will need to adopt in order to become the person you desire to be.

4. Imagine being that person.

ACTIVITY:

1. Make a picture, aging you into the future. Imagine being that future person. What are they doing? Where are they living? What dreams have they made come true? What advice would they give you today?

2. Write down your top 5 goals for the next 12 months. Take a picture of them. Make them the lock-screen on your phone as a reminder several hundred times a day. What you focus on, grows.

3. Make a vision board of all your desires. Post them in your bathroom, bedroom, office, car, refrigerator as a constant reminder of the direction you are moving in.

4. Imagine giving a Ted Talk. What would you say about yourself? About yourself? How you achieved success?

. . .

ACTIVITY:

There are 5 main aspects in our life:

- Career
- Finance
- Health and Wellness
- Relationships
- Romantic Relationships

1. For each aspect, identify all the limiting or negative beliefs you have about it.

2. For each aspect, identify all the limiting or negative beliefs the aspect has about you.

3. Write out a comprehensive list of all the limiting or negative beliefs.

4. Alongside each of the limiting beliefs, re-write them as positive affirmations.

5. Record these and loop them - play them every morning when you get up and every night before you go to bed.

6. As these are impressed on your subconscious, you'll want to repeat the exercise, as you may find new limiting beliefs. Each time I reach a certain threshold, and can't break through it, I do this exercise.

CONCLUSION

Congrats if you've made it this far.

The purpose of this book wasn't to convince you of anything. Only to take you on a journey and enhance your perspective. Expand your awareness.

I think the most important idea in this book, in my opinion is that we have free will over two things and two things only.

1. What we focus on.

2. How we respond or react to circumstances, especially unwanted circumstances.

The old me reacted to unwanted circumstances and then directed my focus to the negative or unwanted parts of my life.

The new me, consciously focuses on the things I desire and consciously responds to unwanted circumstances by redirecting my focus to the wanted, the desired.

Now this takes practice. I'm by no means an expert.

But as I get better so does my life.

The exercises are designed to continuously expand your awareness and deepen your imagination.

I use the same tools anytime I feel stuck or hit a plateau in my goals.

As I use them, I'm able to find the limiting beliefs that are holding me back and eliminate those so I can continuously Level Up.

For example, I hit a plateau recently in my income. I am earning more and more every month than I ever have, but I hit a plateau and I couldn't break through it. I did this exercise on what I believe about my monthly financial goal and then what my monthly financial goal believes about me, and I found that I had a belief that money abandons me. When I looked back at my finances, I found that there was a threshold that I allowed in my bank account. Once I hit that, my sales would start to dwindle or my expenses would begin to increase.

I've done this exercise at least a dozen times and this limiting belief never presented itself before. The beauty in this tool is that it works every time, and it gives me an opportunity to focus on changing the negative or limiting belief.

I have power over my life by having the ability to identify those limiting beliefs and smash them.

In order to be successful at any goal, you have to get brutally honest with yourself. Your ego and your pride need to leave the room, otherwise you're going to remain stuck.

When I started my journey in transforming my life, I made a promise to myself. I promised that when I figured out how to do it and turn my own life around, I would then teach and help others do it.

I fumbled around a lot. I got lost a bit. Spent a lot of time and money on books, courses, coaches, etc. trying to find the best way. In the process, I've been able to build the best strategy to date, for transformation.

This book is the compilation of my findings. I've created a life I'm proud of.

I live in my truth and my purpose.

I wake up fulfilled, loved and happy every single day, and wish the same for all of you.

I love you.

You got this.

Keep going!

Robin

XO XO XO

ABOUT THE AUTHOR

ROBIN DAVIS

Robin Davis is the CEO of Life Mastery with Robin. She is an entrepreneur and mindset coach. She uses tarot, reiki, meditation, and hypnosis to intuitively lead her followers to their highest possible timeline, realizing all their desires.

She believes we are all the God of our own reality and through our thoughts and feelings, we direct the path we walk on.

Robin spent 10 years in the United States Marine Corps, holds a Bachelor's degree in Business Management – Accounting and has had a successful career with several companies prior to building her own business.

She believes becoming your truest, most authentic self is the key to living the life you desire.

Robin currently lives in Denver, Colorado and spends her free time traveling.

Website: https://www.lifemasterywithrobin.com/home
Email: lifemasterywithrobin@gmail.com
Instagram: Life Mastery with Robin
TikTok: Life Mastery with Robin

RESOURCES AND REFERENCES

RESOURCES:
You can find the Activities and additional resources on my website, including '300 TOP Self-Concept Affirmations' (free).
https://www.lifemasterywithrobin.com/book

REFERENCES
1. Plato's allegory of the cave: https://faculty.washington.edu/smcohen/320/cave.htm
2. Scale of Consciousness - Dr, David R. Hawkins, Power vs. Force; I adapted the Scale of State of Being from this
3. Reality Transurfing suggests. (Vadim Zeland - Reality Transurfing).
4. Maslow's Needs: https://canadacollege.edu/dreamers/docs/Maslows-Hierarchy-of-Needs.pdf
5. James Clear's book, Atomic Habits, (highly recommend this book), he introduces Tiny Gains - see picture.

6. Self-Confidence Formula: Napoleon Hill in Think and Grow Rich, published 1937. p. 52-3

7. From Mel Robbins book '5 Second Rule

8. Dr Hew Len, physician in Hawaii

CONTACT Robin

You can reach me via email on this website link or by my Facebook pages and other social media links here.

https://www.lifemasterywithrobin.com/book

Printed in Great Britain
by Amazon